ROADSTER

ROADSTER

How (and Especially Why) a Mechanical Novice

Built a Sports Car from a Kit

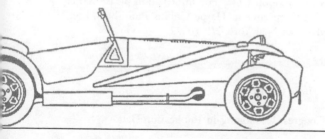

CHRIS GOODRICH

HarperCollins*Publishers*

HarperCollins books may be purchased for educational, business, or sales promotional use. For information please write: Special Markets Department, HarperCollins Publishers, Inc., 10 East 53rd Street, New York, NY 10022.

FIRST EDITION

Designed by Alma Orenstein

Library of Congress Cataloging-in-Publication Data

Goodrich, Chris, 1956–
    Roadster : how (and especially why) a mechanical
novice built a sports car from a kit / by Chris Goodrich. —
1st ed.
        p.   cm.
   ISBN 0-06-019193-7
   1. Automobiles, Home-built—Popular works.   I. Title.
  TL240.2.G66   1998
629.222—dc21   98-17942

---

98 99 00 01 02 RRD/❖ 10 9 8 7 6 5 4 3 2 1

To my parents,

for encouraging me to follow my own road

"Then I wish I had a big red car,"
said Little Bear.
"I would go fast, fast.
I would come to a big castle.
A princess would come out and say,
'Have some cake, Little Bear,'
and I would have some."

ELSE HOLMELUND MINARIK,
LITTLE BEAR

ACKNOWLEDGMENTS

Many people contributed to the making of this volume, some unintentionally. For that reason a few names have been changed, an alteration I hope will be perceived with more relief than annoyance. To those who helped me knowingly I owe many thanks . . . and apologize to those I have unthinkingly left out.

Thanks to Rafe Sagalyn, for encouragement in the early going, and to Ethan Kline, John Jerome, Sonja Bolle, and David Owen, in the later; to Rob Cohen, Chris Tchórznicki, and my parents, for validations literary, technical, and familial; David Bredemeier, for letting me drive his Seven, and J. R. Mitchell for bearing with me; to Carol Mann and Christie Fletcher, for suggesting Henry Dunow; to Mark Darlington and his friend Chris, for their automotive insight; to Bruce Clark of Six of One, for sending a Seven tape; to Cole Coleman and Tony Dangerfield, for their inspiration and recollection.

Special thanks to my brother John and his wife, Jenny, for letting me squat in their garage for more than a year; to Hugh Van Dusen, my editor at HarperCollins, who found interest in oddness; and to Henry Dunow himself, without whom this book, very likely, wouldn't exist.

And extraordinary thanks, finally, to Lisa Miles, and our children Thea and Matthew and Hayley, to whom it was always (okay, usually) a pleasure to return after a long day under the car or at the keyboard. Lisa went far beyond the call of spousal duty, as always being my first, last, and most demanding editor.

Nine in the morning, and the air at the drivers' meeting is already rank. The August sky still threatens rain; it had come down in buckets the night before, but the pit-lane conference room would have felt small and close on the driest day. Those present, all members of the Lotus owners' club, listen intently as a Lime Rock Park driving instructor takes us through the course. It's shaped like a hitchhiker's fist: Big Bend, the track's upraised thumb; the Esses, beginning in the thumb's webbing; No-Name Straight, along the clenched knuckles; Uphill Turn, down the edge of the palm, until Back Straight and West Bend take you to the wrist; and Diving Turn, the palm's heel, where drivers pour on the gas before hitting the long straightaway that ends abruptly, alarmingly, back at Big Bend.

The instructor outlines the best line through the course, noting simultaneously that the line is, for the moment, theoretical. The track is wet, and some of the prescribed turning points, or apexes, are underwater; hit a puddle and you'll likely end up among the weeds and frogs and waterbugs on the other side of the asphalt ... muddy, black-flagged, track privileges possibly suspended. The instructor emphasizes that racing other cars will also lead to a black flag, but the men in the room—there are no women—realize in their bones that by the end of the day, when fear of the unknown has given way to unwarranted confidence, the competitive juices will be flowing, irresistible.

We turn in our tech-inspection sheets, ask a few trivial questions, and divide into groups according to self-proclaimed ability. The instructors offer additional bits of wisdom: More accidents occur on car-club days than any other, if you feel good going into a turn you probably aren't driving it correctly, aim directly at a car that spins out in front of you because it "won't be there by the time you are."

The Connecticut sky now shows patches of blue. The track has begun to dry, but the air in the room remains thick and gamy, old and sweaty, spiked with anxiety and impatience and excitement. Says one driver, putting on his helmet as he proceeds to the infield, past a score of waiting roadsters with their headlights taped and spare wheels removed, "Too much testosterone."

INTRODUCTION

It's hazy, now, those days thirty-odd years ago when I seemed to play with cars—Dinky, Schuco, Matchbox, Corgi, Hot Wheels, the list goes on—all the time. They dashed along electrical tracks or haphazardly after being wound up and released; they ran on their own after an initial push, or required constant manual coaxing. How they progressed didn't really matter, though, for the important thing was that they *moved*, raced from point A to point B at a good clip. It was very gratifying to watch—and still is, as I've noticed while playing with my own children. The message was transparent: *Change is possible*, easy even; just find the right button, the right method, the right moment, and your individual powers can be realized in the world at large. You see a child playing with a toy car, whether it sits atop a pencil or cruises down the sidewalk, and you know, instinctively and immediately, what he or she is thinking: *Someday I'm going somewhere. . . .*

Then we grow up and discover our childish daydreams are just that. Life isn't a highway (as one pop song has it), let alone a freeway; for nearly everyone it's a series of obstacles, in the shape of tests and interviews, bosses and assignments, special needs and empty wallets. And the biggest obstacle of all, of course, is the limitations of talent: the talents we don't have, and those we do but the culture doesn't value. As children we are all potential, all incipient talent, and the world our oyster; we can become anything we want—firefighter, engineer, doctor, pilot, dancer, singer, pro athlete—or so our parents tell us. By adolescence, though, we have watched life's roads close down around us, seen that there are certain things, many things, we simply cannot do.

Young adulthood forces us to make choices, to select an appropriate occupation. And for a time we pursue it contentedly ... until we recognize that open roads, in life, are the exception rather than the rule. We come to roadblocks and detours when we least expect them, find ourselves on dirt roads and in dead ends even after consulting maps; end up lost, turned around, in alien territory. We've been led astray by our own desires, by social and professional pressure, by familial expectations, by the dumb, banal accidents of existence—and it's not always easy to get back on track.

On a personal level, of course, we already knew that trials and troubles await us. That major fight with the parents, that first unrequited crush, that nasty lover's breakup; all make plain that we are never free agents, that hearts and spirits commonly disagree. Yet we seem to assume, when embarking upon a career, that the world of work will treat us better, because it's more rational, less emotionally charged, even—in ideal form—a meritocracy. We work, time goes by, we work more, and more ... and then the rude shock arrives: Labor, of almost every kind, carries veiled, unexpected compromises. We become specialized, compartmentalized, narrowed in mind and perspective almost before knowing it; we grow slowly unrecognizable to ourselves, find our talents overextended or underutilized, distorted or disdained. The child's *Someday I'm going somewhere* is father to the adult's *I'm stuck*, the boundless freedom symbolized by cars having evolved into the everyday experience of grown-up gridlock.

This is one road to the prototypical midlife crisis—the failed promise of the working career—and it is a cultural as well as a personal phenomenon.

When I told friends that I had decided, in my middle thirties, to build by hand a street-legal roadster, many suggested I was too young to be going through a midlife crisis. I agreed, for that wasn't how I saw the project: I pictured it as a great adventure, a break from fifteen years of writing and editing and reporting, the opportunity to learn some skills completely foreign to my professional existence. As time went on, though, I realized that the comment, intended humorously, held more than a grain of truth. It captured something I was loath to admit: that my working life was much less than I wanted it to be. I had held responsible positions, earned the respect of my peers, made a name for myself in (minor) professional circles . . . and yet something was missing.

That something? Joy. Of discovery, of open doors, of seeing the world in new ways; of living in the moment; of following your bliss, as mythologist Joseph Campbell put it. Surely you could do the work you loved without succumbing to its incidental baggage? Pursue a career without kowtowing to careerism; grow professionally without being professionalized? I would come across, years later, the perfect diagnosis of my work malaise. "In the beginner's mind there are many possibilities," the Zen master Shunryu Suzuki told his students, "but in the expert's there are few."

That was the problem in a nutshell: At work I was no longer a beginner, no longer infused with hope and anticipation. The thrill was gone: I knew all too well the formulas of my profession, the reporter's codes, the critic's feints, the writer's strategies. Worse, I sensed daily how my working life had taken over my existence, to the point that it colored most things I saw, felt, thought, did, believed. Every trip was a potential story; every phone call a potential lead; every party a chance to self-promote; every off-beat news item a magazine article awaiting expansion. My working life exerted such gravitational pull on new facts, new events, that I no longer took in the world as it plainly was—a disturbing perception for anyone, but an alarming one for a journalist.

I had been professionalized, expertized, to the point that my working identity strained out elements incompatible with my career—identified them as extraneous, or rearranged, even deformed them to render such particulars harmless. On the surface I seemed to have much greater control over my life, but in my gut I was conscious of being channeled into a limited, enervated way of interpreting experience.

So I built a car.

It was a brash act, a visceral declaration of independence. The kit required no understanding of journalistic narrative, color, balance; indeed, such knowledge would actively impair the car's assembly, for it interfered with what the kit required most: attention to the physical, unmediated present, the here and now. Reporters spend their days looking for compelling stories and credible analysis, writers for just the right word and tone; the kit-car builder, by contrast, carries out the laws of nature, of mechanics, as embodied in steel and rubber and reinforced plastic. It proved a wonderful exchange, trading in abstract ideas for concrete objects, subjective interpretation for objective measurement.

But the beginner's mind is difficult to retain. Soon you're getting ahead of yourself: anticipating the next step, applying tried-and-true methods, looking for patterns, and hoping to predict the future . . . when your basic goal, beneath all that, should be just *paying attention.*

Why the relapse? Because order reassures, experience resonates, because knowledge promises control. The unknown forces you to retreat to familiar skills, makes you go with native strengths; inspires the intruder to reach for his favorite

hammer . . . at which point the world seems a swath of protruding nails. Sad but true, and probably unavoidable: The
very act of exploring kills the unknown, impales the new-
world butterfly on the traveler's old-world pin.

My hammer, my pin, was the written word. And that
meant reading books, lots of them . . . which in turn meant
discovering—here's the silver lining to the cloud of old
methodology—that the automobile was largely responsible
for the specialized, balkanized, expertise-dominated world I
longed to flee. It was Henry Ford, after all, who turned millions of workers into wage slaves through the hyperdivision of
labor, by championing mass production and its counterpart,
mass consumption; it was General Motors' Alfred Sloan who
introduced modern corporate management and the "organization man," who legitimized planned obsolescence and
frivolous styling. In building the car I had uncovered, accidentally on purpose, the taproot of my professional discomfort.

But something else as well. A lateral root—one belonging
to an alternative work culture, for the car I built was antithet-
ical to the modern automobile, its manufacturing process,
indeed the entire car business. The Caterham Super Seven,
based on a 1957 Lotus design, is a deliberately primitive vehicle; handmade, proudly unadorned, self-consciously fundamental, the car both embodies and repudiates its industrial
ancestry. The Seven presumes that the driver and the
mechanic are one and the same, as did Ford's Model T; insists
on being understood, accepted, on its own terms. To drive a
Seven is to celebrate the freedom and functionality of the
automobile while simultaneously criticizing the gigantism and
excess to which it played midwife.

The Seven is thus a mass of (dare I say it) built-in contra-
dictions. And that was, ultimately, its greatest attraction for me
personally, because the car wove together numerous, seemingly incompatible threads of my own life. A family tendency

toward reading and study and intellectualism; a close friendship with an amateur bike and car mechanic who had earned a
doctorate in classics; a passion for the cult television show *The
Prisoner*, in which a disillusioned spy tries to escape from a
homogenized, mind-controlling dystopia. Add car building to
these elements and you have the template for my urge to perceive the world from a fresh angle, to break free of orthodox
interpretation. I wasn't conscious of my motivations at the
time—if I had been, I wouldn't have needed to examine
them—but knew just enough to follow a troublesome desire.

Number Six, the hero of *The Prisoner*, is locked away in a
dystopia called The Village because he refuses to be "pushed,
filed, stamped, indexed, briefed, debriefed, or numbered." But
he *is*, of course, as everyone is, against all protest, who hopes
to play a role in shaping human culture. I'm doubtless subject
to a similar process when I drive my Seven—typed as *that too-
old man in the too-small car*, or as *newly divorced, out to pick up
girls*—and admit to subversive delight in such mischaracteri-
zation; I'm a rolling illustration that you can't judge a book by
its cover. By the same token, though, a surprising number of
people know that the Seven is a kit car, that it possesses a distinguished history, that it represents freedom more than
money to burn, independence more than thrill seeking.

When I climb into the Seven I'm a child again, a beginner
once more. The car tells me, through its carburetor blat and
squeaking springs and growling differential, that I'm *going
nowhere on purpose, with no purpose;* that I've learned through my
hands, in my marrow, that the journey, made rich by attentive-
ness and appreciation, matters far more than the destination.

ALL THE PARTS THAT FIT

We were in some godforsaken section of Boston, down by the port, the roads filled with trucks and the landscape with litter. The doctor, in his early thirties, was picking up special wheels for his recently completed Seven, and to me he was the voice of experience; I was in a near panic, about to take delivery of my Seven crates, anxious to hear that anyone could build one. We small-talked on the loading dock while Chris Tchórznicki, our kit-car mentor and Caterham Cars' best-known U.S. dealer, pursued the shipping and customs paperwork.

I eventually asked how the Seven build went.

"Not so bad," the doctor replied, "though there were all these pieces left over."

I laughed, recognizing the oldest gag in the kit-builder's

vocabulary. Then I looked over and realized the doctor wasn't kidding; his workbench, upon the Seven's completion, really was strewn with uninstalled parts. Was the guy concerned? No, the car ran fine, he said, though the car's top end wasn't what he'd like.

The leftovers? "Nuts and bolts, you know, washers mainly." Nothing, in short, that seemed critical.

I gulped, for him, for me, for every Boston-area driver. And for the accident-prone: Hadn't he said something about being an emergency-room surgeon?

Chris returned a couple of minutes later, followed by a forklift carrying an enormous wooden crate. My name was written on the side in black marker; the adventure had well and truly begun, and I was . . . absolutely not ready. As we maneuvered the first of four crates into the rented truck—they fit with inches to spare, Chris knew the minimum requirements by heart—I found myself wishing I could turn back the clock. *If only I could wake up from this* shit-I-forgot-to-study-for-the-test *nightmare...*

That, or maybe the snow, just beginning to fall, would pile up in record amounts. Let's see: get on I-95, drive a few miles, sling the steering wheel hard right near a rest stop, and my troubles would be over, or at least different (I'd taken out plenty of insurance). Sergeant Doyle to Officer Brown, screeching to a halt before hundreds of Seven parts scattered across the freeway: "Jesus, Mary, and Joseph, if the car's like this I don't want to see the driver. . . "

As it turned out, I arrived at my brother's house in Hastings-on-Hudson, where I planned to build the Seven, without incident. (I managed, at one point, to fill the truck's gas tank with kerosene rather than diesel, but that's another story.) Physical incident, at least: I had spent every hour behind the wheel berating myself for my grand, dazzling, idiotic, fantastical plans. Was I mechanically inclined? Not particularly. Footloose? No, happily married with a two-year-old daughter. A thrill seeker, a daredevil? Possibly, I lived in New York City. An automobile aficionado? Doubtful: I had driven exactly one sports car before, my uncle's red, late-'60s Alfa-Romeo Spider . . . and gotten hit by a Toyota, my first and only accident in fifteen years of driving.

So what was I doing, backing this huge truck containing a million pieces of expensive roadster up my brother John's driveway (and right into the garage door, permanently customizing it)? Trying to prove something to myself, naturally: but what? The question haunted me for the next fourteen months, a time filled with horrible frustrations, unnerving delays, great dollops of fear, enormous satisfaction, and astounding adrenaline rushes. And I suppose that's the answer right there: I built the Seven to experience the highs, and lows, one doesn't get in daily life. Building a car was my sabbatical from the workaday world; and the worst thing about it—even as I threatened to quit the project every week in fury with a recalcitrant part, in fear of decapitation by a falling chassis—was the knowledge that, one day, I'd be finished.

I wish I could say I put months of research into kit cars before settling on a Seven. There are certainly many kits to choose from: knock-offs of classic Mercedes, old Cords, Shelby Cobras (the most popular U.S. kit, by far); variations on Italian exotics and domestic muscle cars; "rebodies" of common sedans and cheap imports. Some are good machines, even excellent, but most are not; the kit-car industry as a whole has been notorious (though less so today) for carnival-barker sales tactics, deceptive easy-pay financing schemes, poor quality control, and frequent bankruptcies. For years such practices were condoned because kit cars represented the off-price, factory-seconds segment of the automobile industry; nobody expected much of a VW-based dune buggy, and rightly so.

The typical customer was a do-it-yourselfer, mechanically self-educated, loaded with dreams but little cash . . . and he usually got what he paid for, which wasn't much.

That's one reason I decided to build a Caterham Seven—because the company had manufactured the car, and nothing else, for more than a quarter century. A number of firms have developed roadsters that resemble the Seven, but only Caterham's is authorized; it bought the manufacturing rights from Lotus, Ltd., in 1973, meaning that Caterham has produced the Seven longer than the car's creator. Once Lotus's mainstay, the Seven had become the company's bottom-of-the-line model by the early '70s, yet thousands of people couldn't bear its demise—among them Graham Nearn, principal owner of the suburban London dealership that sold more Sevens than anyone. Caterham took over the Seven in order to save the car, and it has been a labor of love. Nearn still runs the company, his office yards from the shop floor; his son Robert is a leading driver on Britain's Seven racing circuit.

The Seven is a quality kit, no question. But well-designed, well-integrated components are only the beginning; many people abandon half-finished cars simply because they can't get decent advice during the assembly process. Once the check clears, many kit-car sellers are strangely uninterested in returning telephone calls. That became, consequently, my litmus test: whether I felt I could trust Chris Tchórznicki (pronounced "Chor-NIT-ski"), at that time Caterham's sole U.S. distributor. I stopped by his shop in Cambridge, Massachusetts—he's since moved to a rural Boston suburb, Ayer—for a look-see.

Chris's garage was the antithesis of what you're supposed to look for in an automotive establishment. Tucked away in the corner bay of an old horse stable, the shop was so cluttered it looked like ground zero of a minor explosion.

"Goddam Jensen Healey, those things are a pain in the arse."

So Chris greeted us, by way of explaining what that car was doing in a business called Sevens & Elans. "Doing a fellow a favor," continued Chris in his English accent, the "fellow" being one of Chris's many racing buddies; that was the main reason he started the shop, to subsidize his passion for vintage auto racing. I didn't know about Chris's mania at the time—which was just as well, for otherwise I might have picked up on his (surely significant) skepticism. *This guy lives in Manhattan, he brings along his wife and toddler to check out a racing car?!?*

Chris gave us a tour, which basically meant sweeping an arm across his tiny domain; you had to sidestep constantly to dodge fenders and body panels hanging from the rafters, and step lively to avoid tripping over the heavy-duty parts and tools scattered about the floor. Not that you could see the floor: Most of it was taken up by two Sevens in different stages of assembly. When I put down my daughter, Thea, to take a closer look, she decided to do the same—and made a beeline for the nearest driver's seat (*just my size!*), having noted, no doubt, that the car had no doors. Lisa stopped her in the nick of time.

Lisa looked after squirming Thea, no easy task, while Chris filled me in on the Seven's recent technological history.

"Sixteen-inch wheels, nicer than those," said Chris, pointing to a set coated with brake-shoe dust. "The new pattern's more attractive. And look here"—gesturing inside a Seven's engine bay—"a few years back they changed the ignition timing to take unleaded fuel. Also upgraded the radiator, lightened the fuel tank. The car passed the European Community's barrier tests, too." The implication was clear: Even though Caterham sold only about eight hundred kits and fully assembled Sevens a year, it was getting close to producing a "world car."

The new model, the one I was considering, had further

refinements. "Look at that," said Chris, indicating the front suspension on his demonstrator Seven. "It's been redesigned: double-wishbones, eliminates the trunnion, it's a much more elegant setup. The roll bar's better anchored, slotted in rather than bolted on; the chassis itself is lighter, same with the De Dion tube. They design everything on the computer now, play around with components to shave weight."

Chris tapped the car's aluminum-clad side. "Honeycomb panels, they make the car more rigid and safer." He pointed behind the seats but ahead of the spare wheel, where a boxy depression could hold, maybe, two well-compressed sleeping bags. "And the boot's slightly bigger this year."

There was one more significant change—the horn, after thirty-one years on the dashboard, had finally been moved to the steering-wheel hub. It was a long-delayed improvement, certainly, but highlights the fact that Caterham, unlike most U.S. car manufacturers (until recently), actually listens to customers. It may take a while, but problems with the Seven are solved rather than swept under the carpet. Overheating? Add a cooling-fan shroud. Rust problems? Give the chassis an epoxy-powder coating. Too cramped for long-legged drivers? Move the chassis's seat support toward the rear of the car (an improvement made possible by the installation of a smaller differential). Caterham, in contrast to Lotus and some other old-school carmakers, fixes flaws rather than abandons the troubled model.

Chris walked us over to a Seven he was about to complete. It was a beauty—a re-creation, down to the metal-mesh headlight guards and red-leather bench seat, of the car that makes cameo appearances in *The Prisoner*. Green body and yellow nose, like the great Lotus racers; white piping on the black boot cover, like Number Six's Village uniform; chrome instrument bezels and stainless-steel brake hoses, all very snazzy. The car nearly took my breath away, especially after Chris said he was assembling this particular Seven for Patrick McGoohan, the star, producer, and sometime writer/director of *The Prisoner*. Payment for McGoohan's giving his blessing to Caterham's Limited Edition Prisoner Series Super Seven, the car was assembled—of course—on Chassis No. Six.

The Prisoner Seven was one to lust over—but it cost $22,995, without an engine. It might even have been a good investment, but the "limited" designation seemed to mean (in lopsided Lotus fashion) only that Caterham would cease production when customers stopped ordering. *The Prisoner* Seven's biggest selling point, in retrospect, was its making the standard edition seem, at $18,500, almost a bargain.

"It's not a family car," said Lisa wryly as we drove home, having strapped our daughter into the rented Ford. "And where'd Thea's seat go?"

"What," I said defensively, "you want me to build a sedan? A station wagon? I don't think they make those as kits." That was an out-and-out lie. "Besides, do you want Thea riding in a car I made myself?"

"Well, maybe not." Lisa paused. "So, do you think you're gonna do it?"

"I'm tempted. I mean, $18,000, that's not so bad, if you can get it back when you sell the car."

"But could you? Sell it, that is? Some guy buys the car, a few months later he has an accident and he says there was some mechanical problem. You're the builder, right? Could he . . . "

"Let's not think about it," I said. And tried not to, hard.

Back in New York I looked up *trunnion* in my newly acquired auto books. None, amazingly, mentioned the word in their indices, but Webster's New Collegiate came through: "either of two opposite gudgeons on which a cannon is swiveled." Ah, I should've known. And *gudgeon*? "A small European freshwater fish," or alternatively, "a socket for a rudder pintle."

This was going to be fun . . . or, quite possibly, not.

Here's P. J. O'Rourke, of all people, in *House & Garden*, of all publications, writing about the Caterham Super Seven in 1987: "a godawful car, and more fun than spending the whole Jazz Age in Paris. . . . If there were any less Caterham, you'd be sitting alone in the street."

The Seven seems to bring out the best in automobile writers. I'm not sure why, exactly, but it must have something to do with the car's coming so close to perfecting a concept that's inherently imperfectable. The English are famous for their two-seat roadsters—Morgans, MGs, Lotuses, Jaguars, Healeys, TVRs, Sunbeams, Triumphs, and so on—and to a car they are idiosyncratic, demanding, unreliable, and often ornery. And here's the funny thing: They are beloved not in spite of those characteristics but because of them, because they are half-executed theories incomplete without their drivers.

The roadster driver doesn't feel like the mindless operator of a complex machine but an integral part of it, always in touch with its motions, its tendencies, its fears and enthusiasms. A roadster doesn't dehumanize its owner; the owner humanizes the roadster, man and machine searching together for a happy compromise between their disparate natures. And nowhere is that compromise more agreeable, it seems, than in the Seven.

Automobile magazines are not the most reliable sources, but few carmakers—not Porsche, not BMW, not Alfa-Romeo, not Ferrari, not Rolls-Royce—have produced the kind of zealotry and affection that Lotus and Caterham have with the Seven. A sampling, in generally chronological order:

Sports Car Illustrated, 1960: "as spartan and unadorned as a rowboat"; entering the car in winter is "like climbing into a frozen sleeping bag with a wooden leg."

Autosport, 1961: "The Super Seven is so low that one sometimes trips over it in the dark. . . . You need an extra pullover or two when the nights are cold. If you mind about this sort of thing, this car is too good for you. . . ."

Road & Track, 1962, in contrast to some of the more forgiving British reviews: "Heat pours into the cockpit. Even though we expect a certain amount of discomfort with a machine like this, the Super Seven on several occasions gave us the distinct impression that it was really on fire."

Sports Car World, 1964: "the look of a praying mantis, the comforts of a gaol cell. . . . At speed the Super Seven attracts more draught than a medieval castle."

Road & Track, 1968: "Driving with the top up is comparable to riding inside a bass drum."

Motor Sport, 1970: "clings to the road like a limpet and steers with the accuracy of a micrometer." (The magazine had changed its mind by 1985, when the reviewer wrote, "Nobody could call the rear end traction 'limpet-like': it is fairly easy to spin the car in the dry.")

Road & Track, 1970: "One clambers over the side and inserts feet, rather like putting on a bag of golf clubs. Driving on rough pavement is like being strapped to a jackhammer."

Car and Driver, 1971: A headline reads, "If you think of it as a car, you will be disappointed," but the author goes on to call the Seven "about the best handling car I've ever driven" (and to note that the seats "bite down on your pelvis like an enraged giant clam").

Autocar, 1973 and 1978, respectively: "This brutal, forgiving, funny, frightening little vehicle"; "It doesn't accelerate so much as explode off the line."

Fast Lane, 1984: "a thoroughly uncompromising beast that won't be adapted to suit you, you have to come to terms with it. . . . a little rocket ship."

Road & Track, 1984: "Tiny, shaped like a flattened torpedo inspired by alloy cigar box. . . ."

Motor Sport, 1985, on getting in: "Given the contortions involved, had I had a lady already in the passenger seat, the only decent thing would be to have married her."

Motor, 1985: "At 3000 revs it sounds like a Spitfire (Battle of Britain variety) and at 5000 you're being chased by a whole squadron. Release the accelerator, and the exhaust mimics a popcorn machine."

Graham Arnold, long-time Lotus marketing director, in *The Illustrated Lotus Buyer's Guide*, 1986: "The Seven is a car with no real creature comforts, an apology for a heater, water leaks everywhere and luggage space enough for a bikini and two toothbrushes"; "Carry a large fire extinguisher."

Automobile, 1988: "a driving position that would shame a wooden folding chair."

Fast Lane, 1990: "The Caterham felt like Superman unable to find a telephone box to change back into his Clark Kent persona."

Classic and Sportscar, 1991: "a wonderful cocktail of exhilarating performance, brilliant handling, complete exposure to the elements, cheeky looks and simple mechanicals."

Road & Track, 1991: "There are no mechanical limitations, only those of conscience and public safety."

Sports Car International, 1992: "Progress out of bends could be twitchy, even alarming, like wrestling with an agitated alligator."

Car and Driver, 1993: "This car looks like something Porky Pig might drive in a Warner Brothers cartoon. . . . Sometimes the package seems so goofy, it's hard to stop grinning."

Automobile, 1994: "It reacts in a manner that is almost telepathic. . . . Cars don't get much lower than this, so you risk getting the cocked-leg treatment from passing dogs."

Could any red-blooded male resist such effusiveness, such promise, such danger? Not me: I also wanted to experience acceleration as explosion, steering by micrometer, control limited only by moral principle. Youth may indeed be wasted on the young, as George Bernard Shaw said, but adolescence is positively squandered on adolescents; they don't have the personal knowledge that renders significant the ability to escape, to reject, to renounce with earned conviction.

I wrestled with that $18,500 figure for weeks, attempting to justify it, defeat it, outflank it. A whole lot more than the earnings of my first paying job, selling ads extremely part-time at a magazine about West Coast publishing; a fair bit less than my starting salary at *California Lawyer,* way back in 1982; the same, practically, as the advance on my first book; an outlay that would feed entire families for a decade or more in some parts of the world. Yes, written in a checkbook it represented a ton of money, but in others ways seemed a drop in the bucket. When compared to real-estate investing, for example—which I had done years earlier, by accident, and which allowed me to write the aforementioned check, to Chris, with only a few involuntary twitches.

Maybe it's true that behind every fortune lies a crime (credit the line to Balzac). I don't know of any major offenses committed by my ancestors—if we don't count, as we should, the age-old water misappropriations in southern California—but there's certainly crime in my personal history. It's not the variety, though, Balzac had in mind.

One evening, while living in Oakland, California, I bought a coffee-table art book at the local bookstore. The neighborhood, adjacent to a major and relatively upscale (for Oakland) commercial district, was considered safe, but residents were cautious after dark nevertheless; our downstairs neighbor had been raped a few months earlier, and criminals as well as customers flocked to the local bank's new ATM. Sometimes, of course, those categories were indistinguishable; a friend in San Francisco swore by his local ATM, regularly arriving at a North Beach machine just before midnight on Fridays, thus able to get two days' cash—one $100 withdrawal at 11:59 P.M., a second at 12:01 A.M.—with which to feed his cocaine habit.

So I was concerned, but not overly so, when I heard footsteps suddenly starting up behind me. I lived on the street, and indeed could see the lights were on in my apartment—Cheryl was back from campus.

"Do what I tell you muthafucker or I'll blow your muthafuckin head off. You see this?" I turned my head to the sound; something glinted in a proffered hand. "Look straight ahead, muthafucker, don't look round or ya dead. Don't fuck with me."

I did as the boy said—and he was a boy, about fourteen, judging from his size and voice. He took my arm firmly and guided me to the back steps of the three-story house next to mine. He told me to hand over my wallet.

For a nanosecond I considered struggling, as I wasn't entirely convinced I had seen a gun. On the other hand, I had just spent most of my cash, and the boy seemed at least semiprofessional (if hyperactive). I'd be fine, I thought, if he didn't panic, and I figured he wouldn't panic if I didn't first.

"What's your number?" he asked, rifling through my wallet.

"My number? . . . I don't know, I, I, my Social Security number . . . "

"Don't fuck with me, muthafucker. Your bank-card number."

Relieved, I made one up.

"Say it again."

I did, and fortunately was able to repeat the charade.

He took his time going through the wallet. He even patted me down, like a cop looking for weapons, for reasons I never understood. Perhaps I kept credit cards in my socks?

"Put your arms behind your back and kneel down."

I did what he said, shocked, disbelieving. Execution style, in the movies at least. No point now, is there?

"Don't move for ten minutes or ya dead. I'm gonna watch." And he was gone.

It might have been ten minutes, or five that seemed like ten, but when I stood up I was alone. In two minutes I was back in my apartment telling Cheryl what had happened; within the hour I was talking to the police, unable to give them even a sketchy description of my mugger. The next day I was back at work, refusing to take time off, as my boss suggested—I felt safer at work now than at home.

The next evening I gave my parents the details. The following week they offered to give me and Cheryl the down payment on a house in a truly safe neighborhood, and a few months later—having discovered, to our surprise, that we'd have to break the $100,000 barrier—we accepted their proposal. It was a small, lovely house in the Berkeley hills, one with a cracked foundation and an amazing view of San Francisco Bay (for which we gladly gave up our hoped-for third bedroom). The house doubled in value within five years, making it by far the best investment I've ever made.

I wonder, sometimes, whether my assailant straightened out or whether he's doing hard time in San Quentin. I doubt he ever thinks of me, and never imagines, certainly, that his assault actually freed me from nagging money worries. I had few to begin with—my parents were prosperous—but that mugging made money seem, well, beside the point. It came, it went, and sometimes, as that now-ancient assault demonstrated, money came precisely because it went.

So who knew where $18,500 might lead?

To further outlays, as it happened, for the Seven's $18,500 M.S.R.P. proved only the beginning. The figure was bare-bones—and understandably so, looking back, because many buyers, intending to race their Sevens, spurned speed-stealing luxuries like heaters and armrests and wind deflectors. But if you did want a heater, you forked over $157, plus another $52 for its control valve; $68 for the armrest; $71 more for the deflectors. An oil cooler? $150. Seat belts? Required by U.S. law, of course, but still optional to Caterham, at $110 for the standard set, $205 for the four-point racing harness. More necessary options: roll bar ($90), spare wheel spacer ($24), head restraints ($95), twin air horns ($30)—so other drivers can hear you when they can't see you, often the case with the low-slung Seven. The clutch, it should be noted, is included in the base price—which should please former race driver Dan Gurney, who was disgruntled to discover, in the 1960s, that the clutch on his racing Lotus was considered an "optional extra."

And then there's the engine, the most important, most expensive "option" of all. You can provide your own, if you know what you're doing: Refurbished motors are standard procedure among kit-car builders, and Seven racers often drop in Mazda rotaries, or even Detroit V-8s. I was much too fainthearted for that route, though, choosing instead to buy from Caterham the most popular Seven engine, the 1,700cc

SuperSprint. At $4,185 it seemed a steal, at least compared to the Cosworth BDR RS 1700 Twincam, at $10,495, or the two-liter Vauxhall 16-valve Twincam, at $10,395 (after accounting, in the latter's case, for the chassis modifications necessary to accommodate it).

True, the SuperSprint would take 5.8 seconds to reach 60 mph rather than the 5.2 seconds clocked by the Cosworth or the 4.9 by the Vauxhall, but my plain-vanilla Seven would still smoke a few Porsches and Ferraris. Anyway, if acceleration was all-important, I'd have moved to England and splurged on a custom-built Seven JPE; for a time it was the quickest 0–60 production car on earth, getting there in a mere 3.4 seconds. (It was less remarkable at higher speeds, for Sevens are nonaerodynamic in the extreme. One successful racing Seven was affectionately dubbed the "Black Brick"; a later development of the car, sporting air dams and airfoils, was called "Slippery Brick".)

The grand total? Add import duties, customs-broker fees, state taxes, local taxes, and other, unanticipated charges and expenses, and the Seven would cost me, all told, a sticker-shock inducing $27,000. In theory, all those hours devoted to putting the kit together might eventually pay off; in practice, though, it was a sucker's bet. I once asked Chris to describe the worst Seven assembly job he'd seen, and he just laughed and said, "You don't want to know."

2

"EVERY NUT AND BOLT AND COG . . ."

The man on the street is disoriented, distraught, locked out of the London flat from which he'd been kidnapped months earlier. A middle-aged woman pulls up to the front door in a yellow-and-green roadster; it too looks familiar, right down to the license plate.

"What's the number of that car?" the man asks aggressively.

She puts on a patronizing smile and says "Terribly interesting."

"KAR 120C," he replies on her behalf. "What's the engine number?"

"Do tell me," says she.

He rushes on. "461034 TZ."

"Marvelous."

"I know every nut and bolt and cog. I built it with my own hands."

"Then you're just the man I want to see," the woman replies. "I'm having a good deal of overheating in traffic. Perhaps you'd care to advise me. . . ."

The woman's name is Mrs. Butterworth, the man's . . . well, nobody knows. Throughout the seventeen hours of *The Prisoner* he is referred to only as Number Six, but many fans insist he is an older John Drake, the spy played by Patrick McGoohan in his other well-known TV venture, *Secret Agent*. (Johnny Rivers spat out the famous theme song, which includes the line "They've given you a number, and taken 'way your name.") The character's past identity isn't important, however, for what matters in *The Prisoner* is Number Six's constant ability to resist a hostile, seductive, morally bankrupt world, his refusal to go along for the sake of going along.

It was natural, when McGoohan set out to find a car that suited Number Six's personality, to think of Lotus. By the mid-1960s the carmaker was dominating Formula 1 racing, and Diana Rigg, as Mrs. Peel, drove a Lotus Elan in the television series *The Avengers*. Lotus executives insisted McGoohan take a spin in the Seven, and its selection seems preordained: The Seven was "a symbol of all the Prisoner was to represent," as McGoohan said later, "standing out from the crowd, quickness and agility, independence and a touch of the rebel." Not to mention a symbol of *self-reliance;* once you knew Number Six had built his own car, you had no trouble believing he could also, in the course of endless futile attempts to escape The Village, construct sailboats, rafts, compasses, sextants, radios, and so on.

Number Six is abducted and imprisoned, by parties unknown, for no better reason than quitting his job as a secret agent. The abduction is recapitulated in the series' opening sequence, and it is a classic television moment.

A stormy English sky, a powerful thunderclap, an empty roadway dividing a deserted moor; driving toward the viewer, at high speed, a bare-headed man in an open roadster. Squinting in the sunlight, wearing a smile that's both sly and contemptuous, he turns into the bowels of a building shadowed by the Houses of Parliament.

He strides purposefully down a bureaucratic hallway, throws up a restricted-access door, and pounds furiously on a superior's desk (a tea saucer breaks). The man then drives home in his Lotus Seven, unwittingly followed by a black, marqueless hearse, and hurriedly packs. As he does so, his security photograph, back at his former place of employment, is x-ed out in an automatic typewriter and deposited by machine in a file drawer labeled "Resigned."

A white gas sprays through the front-door keyhole; the man passes out on his bed. All appears normal when he awakens . . . until he raises the window blinds and discovers that his flat has been replicated in a strange, beautiful, through-the-looking-glass compound.

Here, in The Village, the man is addressed as Number Six, to which the McGoohan character defiantly retorts, "I am not a number, I am a free man!" *His protest is met with gales of disembodied laughter from "the new Number Two," the Village overseer, who changes with nearly every episode because Number Six somehow finds a way, despite constant surveillance and frequent betrayal, to force the previous Number Two's removal. The ongoing battle between Number Two and Number Six is physical and emotional, psychological and intellectual, and can end only when one of the combatants' questions is answered. Number Two's question is,* Why did you resign?; *Number Six's,* Who is Number One?

The sequence takes on further meaning when you learn that Patrick McGoohan quit *Secret Agent* as Britain's highest-paid television actor. Like Number Six, McGoohan abandoned a seemingly terrific job, a stellar career, in favor of the unknown, hoping to find, in the crucible of *The Prisoner*, something of abiding significance.

Blue-denim work shirt; flannel-lined pants; rag socks; a stained, striped sweater hanging so long in the closet the hook has poked through the collar. I hadn't worn these clothes in a long time—certainly as an ensemble, if you can call it that—because it had been a long time since I'd worked with my hands.

Handiness runs in the family. More on my mother's side than my father's: She grew up in eastern Washington State, wheat and lentil country next to Idaho, where you either farmed or talked with farmers every day. Both of Mom's parents worked, and she did too, for years to make a living but also because, having grown up during the Great Depression, she knew no other way.

Mom has a Ph.D. in sociology from UC Berkeley, and spends most of her free time reading. You wouldn't know it, though, from a casual visit to my parents' home in Santa Barbara, despite the books and bookshelves in every room. What you notice is the lacquered boxes, the elaborately embroidered pillows, the mosaic tabletops, at Christmas the beribboned tree ornaments . . . all emblems of Mom's always-moving hands. Sometimes, in my youth, she'd watch television with the kids, but it was an indulgence, Mom's fret-free luxury while she finished latch-hooking a rug or patching a shirt or seaming a cushion.

My father's pretty handy, too, but not from necessity. He also grew up on agricultural land, but it was the gentleman-farm variety; the orchards surrounding my grandparents' home were valued for producing privacy more than fruit.

There were few chores to do, the house being full of servants, but that suited the family just fine because my paternal grandparents loved, above all, the life of the mind. My father's father was a lawyer, his mother a poet, both were philanthropists, and they encouraged their children to follow their own strengths and needs. Pop's strong suit was academics, so it was nearly inevitable that he ended up with a Ph.D.— though his specialty, classical Chinese language and literature, was undeniably arcane.

Pop earned his doctorate a few years after Mom received hers—World War II delayed his studies—but when the children came, there was no question who would stay home. In many ways Mom had better professional prospects. She had worked her way through college and graduate school as a secretary and lecturer, was naturally gregarious, and in a growing field—but social conventions, even in my father's very progressive family, were as often obeyed as flouted. My grandmother did take her husband's name, for example—but only after acquaintances began asking, "And how are the children, Miss?"

My father needed to work for his own psychological health. He longed, I think, to pay his own way, though didn't get the chance until he approached forty: because of the war, and Berkeley's reluctance to part with a rare graduate student in Chinese, and my father's sense that there was so much more to learn. But a job offer did arrive, a fabulous one: an appointment at Cambridge University. We lived in England for nearly three years, returning just in time for John Kennedy's assassination. The following year Pop accepted a professorship at the virtual antithesis of Cambridge, in culture at least—UC Santa Barbara, where he taught until retirement thirty years later. I vividly remember him complaining about a student who attended a lecture in bare feet, having left his surfboard outside the classroom door.

My father didn't do much plumbing and electrical work around the house, but it wasn't for lack of mechanical skill. It was a question of time, of the hours spent away from his study—wall-to-wall books, a sea of Chinese characters—being hours not spent mastering his field. John and I, on the occasional Saturday, would ask Pop to play fungo, and he usually agreed, but we knew Pop's work came first. He was more accessible in the backyard, yet seemed preoccupied nonetheless, catching up (we assumed) on the academic-journal work shunted aside by his teaching load. Physical work, for Pop, seemed neither a time filler nor a change of pace but an excuse for reflection. Those afternoons he spent, one year, sanding down and varnishing the back-door threshold; the project took forever, as if Pop needed it to last until he'd untied some scholarly knot.

The same strands show up in his children. My three siblings and I have been deeply involved in academics—as graduate students or teachers—but we've been hands-on as well. Especially the boys: David, a custom typesetter specializing in Chinese texts, used to make metal and ceramic jewelry in a kiln and thinks nothing of dismantling computers; John, an artist, former custom cabinetmaker and adult-education instructor, always seems to be tiling a bathroom or making furniture. In many ways I was the black sheep, the least dexterous son, the least imaginative . . . which may explain why I was the only child to get a "real," full-time, stamped-signature-paycheck job.

And also why I left that job, and why I decided to build a car. For wouldn't it be nice to end the day with something solid to touch, as my brothers did? That simple physicality seemed to render journalism, however interesting and respectable, evanescent: for everything I did—sometimes representing months, even years of work—ended up, sooner or later, in the pulping machine.

Lisa's upbringing, by contrast, was hands-off, mostly due to environmental conditioning. It's a foreign concept to most people, I expect, but in Manhattan you use your hands primarily to push buttons to summon the elevator, the superintendent, the doorman, or (by phone) an outside expert. There are few opportunities for manual labor—where's the garden plot? the workshop? the two-car garage? the space for a new deck?—and little incentive to get dirty, take a chance. Why fool with the plumbing yourself, mess with electrics, if the super's available and paid for? And just think: make one mistake and you could have hundreds of neighbors—*New Yorkers*—furious with you.

Handiness was discouraged in Lisa's family, too, by example if nothing else. Her mother left the family farm in Georgia as soon as she could, determined to become an actress; she had a college degree but no backup career when she arrived in New York City, and refused to learn typing so she couldn't be coerced into the secretarial pool (where new-in-town working girls always seem to end up, at least in the movies). Knowing in her bones the dull routine of manual labor, she understood that skills opened the door to workplace ghettos as well as to success.

That was one reason, surely, I was attracted to Lisa—the fact that we had so little in common, that she illuminated my dark corners. And even the major interest we shared—good books—we came at from opposite directions; she was an editor working in the center of the publishing universe (at Harper & Row, coincidentally), while I was an up-from-hackdom writer from the Coast. Deep down, I think, each of us wanted the other's job, having realized the roads we had freely chosen were leading not to professional satisfaction but depressing dead ends. Now if we teamed up . . .

The Seven, uncrated, turned John's garage into a fraternity prank. Car parts were everywhere—tires in one corner, exhaust system in another, transmission box in the middle, carburetor filters and starter motor on a shelf, cables and moldings and hoses and tie-wraps and clamps hanging on the walls . . . not to mention the nails, plastic, tape, newspaper, cardboard, metal frames, rubber, lumber, and other miscellaneous by-products of unpacking. A mess, all in all, but somehow it seemed appropriate that demolition and disassembly should precede construction. You must clear the field, command the landscape, before you grow or build.

Holding the mess together, theoretically at least, was the Seven's assembly manual, clipped into a green, three-ring binder (and not just any green but BRG, British Racing Green). The first task suggested by the manual was taking inventory, which I started the next day. My plan was to work on the car two mornings a week, alternating those six to eight hours with my regular journalism. That way I'd develop, I hoped, a good assembly rhythm but not work on the car so intensely as to get carried away by the thrill of it . . . and thus do something irreparably stupid.

A novice is supposed to be able to put a Seven together in less than a hundred hours, while Chris can do it in something under sixty. Almost immediately, though, I discovered it can take about that long just to catalog the car's seemingly innumerable components. One reason is the absence of a part-by-part shipping statement, but another, I suspect, is Caterham's determination that a Seven builder should give up any sense of control as soon as possible. British roadsters are notoriously unreliable, and while the Seven is more dependable than most, the owner must adapt himself to its requirements. You'd like, say, a dashboard clock? Sheer heresy, for the car is deliberately, and literally, an anachronism, not to be measured by contemporary standards (except, of course, on the track). If you have to ask how many hours it takes to build and maintain a Seven, you can't afford the time.

After uncrating the Seven, I confronted a good many articles that appeared to suit an aircraft better than an automobile. Many parts, of course, I had no trouble identifying. Shocks and springs, brakes and suspension elements, easy; brake lines and oil cooler and air horns, likewise. More problematic were the struts for holding up the fenders and the extremely fragile-looking steering column—you could mistake it for a curtain rod. Particularly satisfying, I found, was determining the function of a few items that the average Joe never thinks about. The starter motor, with its projecting pinion gear; the heater, looking like a stealth-jet prototype (aborted); the rear wheel bearings, wrapped in tissue before being placed in delicate, robin's-egg-blue boxes. Tie a white bow around such a box, hand it to your steady girl after a fine dinner, and chances are she'd murmur *Tiffany!* and melt.

But what was this shiny, metallic blue aquarium pump, (a), wrapped in a San Diego newspaper bearing the headline, "Gorbachev Resigns Post as Party Chief"?

Or this, (b), which resembled nothing so much as a cat toy?

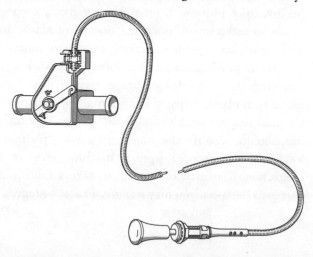

Or this, (c), which could pass for a primitive musical instrument?

Or this, (d), which made me want to go dowsing for water?

The manual's "Parts Recognition Sheet" cleared up a few riddles—so that's *not* a Michael Graves–designed clothes pin, it's a piece of the handbrake linkage!—but these components continued to baffle. [I won't keep you in suspenders: They are, respectively, (a) the hydraulic clutch slave cylinder, (b) the heater valve and switch, (c) the differential breather tube, and (d) the spare wheel spacer.] I put the parts on a high shelf, figuring that the attrition of uninstalled parts would, in due time, make their purpose plain.

Intelligent kit builders would no doubt have completed the inventory process. I, on the other hand, soon gave up, unable to make myself open the dozens of plastic bags corralling nuts, bolts, washers, screws, rivets, grommets, spacers, caps, cotter pins, clamps, *ad infinitum*. I was working in a disorganized, dusty, leaf-laden garage, its dirt floor barely concealed with plastic tarps; if I accidentally dropped something it would unquestionably disappear, at which point I would undoubtedly identify the object as a rare, platinum-plated doodad special-ordered from a machine shop in Finland. That's how I justified my failure to take a full inventory, at least . . . a decision, you may be sure, I came to regret.

3

KEEP IT SIMPLE

The Lotus Seven was unveiled at the Earls Court Motor Show in 1957. It arrived with minimal fanfare: Colin Chapman, founder of Lotus Engineering and the car's designer, was more interested in pushing the new Lotus Elite, an upscale automobile that represented a major break from the company's impoverished, ragtag roots. Lotus wasn't yet ten years old, but Chapman had already concluded that the only way it could become a power in international road racing—his deepest love—was to tap the affluent car-enthusiast market.

The Seven, consequently, was obsolete almost from birth. Chapman had indeed created "the simplest, most basic, lightest, highest performance little car that we could come up with for two people at minimum cost" . . . and with that goal accomplished, he lost interest. "Despite what purists like to think," Lotus's Graham Arnold has written, "Colin Chapman did not care a bit for the Lotus Seven," even though he once called it the firm's "bread-and-butter line." The Seven, come to life, was immediately old hat: Having seen it become a road-going reality, Chapman was ready to begin his next automotive breakthrough.

Chapman developed the Seven to reach the low end of the automobile market. The car was promoted to college students, and many could actually afford it: That first year you could buy the Seven in a showroom for £1,036, or in kit form for £536, because car parts were exempt from Britain's 25 percent purchase tax. This last fact explains why Lotus produced for seventeen years a car its creator didn't particularly like; because Chapman, racing aside, loved nothing more than twitting authority. When a rule barred his way—whether a government regulation, a physical law, a racing convention, or accepted engineering wisdom—Chapman wouldn't rest until he found a way to circumvent it.

And the Seven was a rule-breaker's dream. Under British law, for example, Lotus could not provide kit buyers with professional help, and that included an assembly manual. Chapman's solution? He had at least two. A friendly automotive journalist (a Lotus employee, some believe) published under the byline "Sports Car Fan" a magazine story entitled "How to Build a Lotus Seven"; a buyer equipped with the article didn't need further advice. And there was another guide as well, for the owner's manual contained the equivalent information in the guise of a chapter describing the "rebuilding" of a Seven in the wake of a terrible accident. Such back-door shenanigans earned Chapman numerous antagonists, but only added to Lotus's marketplace allure.

Chapman died of heart failure in 1982 at the age of fifty-four, but his suspicion toward authority lives on. My Seven arrived in the United States without a complete shipping statement because Chris didn't want a gung-ho customs inspector coming across it and deciding that the shipment constituted a complete car. My kit arrived in two batches for the same reason, the chassis and tires in my name on one freighter and the engine, bearing my brother John's name, on another. Although Chris occasionally had problems with the Customs Service, these precautions were more traditional than necessary: They recall the fact that English customers of the 1950s had to buy Seven kits from two different companies—the chassis from Lotus Engineering, the motor from Lotus Engines—to stay legal.

Chapman's fame as an automobile designer—world-champion racer Emerson Fittipaldi called him "simply the best race car engineer in the world"—rests mainly on his accomplishments in two areas: the chassis and the suspension. He was trained as a civil engineer at University College, London, but seems to have learned much more on the job than in the classroom. Throughout his career he stressed lightness, structural rigidity, and aerodynamics (remember, the Seven was an *early* Lotus), characteristics he became intimately familiar with as a Royal Air Force pilot and British Aluminum engineer. He wanted, essentially, to design cars that performed more like airplanes than trucks, an impulse decades ahead of its time.

While Detroit added fins and cowls to make its cars resemble jet fighters, Chapman put genuine aeronautical knowledge into his—though not, be it said, aeronautical reliability. "Of course they break," he liked to say about his notoriously fragile automobiles. "That's all part of Lotus ownership." Caterham, fortunately, doesn't respect that side of the Lotus tradition. The modern Seven's reliability is perhaps best exemplified by its winning, in 1992, a twenty-four-hour road race by going nearly two thousand miles at an average of

85 mph—and beating, in the process, fifty-three other teams running cars like the Mazda RX-7 and the Datsun 240Z. The Seven won by seven laps.

It was fitting, consequently, that the first Seven part I installed was a suspension item—the front shock absorbers. (They are referred to officially as "coil-spring damper units," for it's the springs wrapped around the dampers that absorb road shocks: the dampers prevent the spring from oscillating.) It was some time before I commenced the assembly, however, for the first problem I faced was getting the chassis in a workable position.

"Put it up on a couple of sawhorses, that's a good jig," said Chris. "But cover them up with carpet scraps so you don't nick the chassis epoxy."

Easier said than done.

Although the sawhorses were a cinch—for each I laid shipping-crate lumber across a couple of jack stands—getting the chassis on top of them was a Chaplinesque experience. I could lever, barely, one end of the chassis—which resembled rather too closely an aluminum coffin—onto a carpeted sawhorse, and then hustle down to the other end, still on the ground. But what next? I picked up the lower end, and using my foot, brought the other sawhorse underneath it . . . while every movement, every kick and tap and pull, threatened to tip over the first sawhorse. A see-sawhorse dance developed, with me at one end, leaning this way and then that, deploying a hand on the chassis here and a shoe on the sawhorse there, getting closer and closer to my goal but also, simultaneously, to dropping the chassis on my foot.

There was one consolation—the original, 1950s Seven jig wasn't much better. In fact it was probably worse, being an old iron bedstead. The chassis itself wasn't anything to boast about either: Some of its brackets were cut from old filing cabinets and bread boxes.

But I was learning something, no? Yes—that I was an idiot. For working alone, particularly. Les, my old friend and high-school Latin teacher, who had introduced me to Sevens fifteen years earlier: Why hadn't I insisted he lend a hand, as Les had once volunteered? I had previously been told it takes at least three people to build a Seven: one to do the work, one to kibitz, and one to drink the beer. The kibitzer can double as driver, presumably, when the assembler has to be rushed off to the emergency room.

Persistence eventually paid off. I got the second sawhorse partially under the chassis and managed, after running to the far side and repositioning the first sawhorse, to bump the second all the way under before the whole getup collapsed in a heap.

Great. Ten in the morning and I was already emotionally drained and physically spent. I went inside the house, chatted with my sister-in-law Jenny, made another cup of coffee, and girded my loins. Back in the garage I circled the chassis like a pool player with a bad lie, thinking, yes, searching for an angle . . . and above all delaying, scared of my dangerous, almost willful ignorance. Knowing that as long as I didn't do anything, I couldn't do anything wrong.

The Seven's front suspension, at first glance, seemed complicated. The dampers—Bilsteins, apparently that's good—bolted into a cleft at the base of the lower suspension wishbones, which in turn were bolted to the chassis parallel to the upper wishbones, with the wheel assemblies (stay with me) later mounted upright between the wishbones. "Do not be tempted to use an ordinary hammer to help line up the [damper] mountings," the manual helpfully cautioned, but positioning them wasn't my problem; tightening was. I didn't have an Allen wrench big enough to fit the damper bolts' hex-head recesses.

Twenty minutes into the build and I was off to Hastings

Hardware . . . and returning a pissed-off, grease-monkey Goldilocks, having discovered that of the fourteen wrenches in my new Allen set, none were just right. Was I dealing with metric rather than standard bolts, or, God forbid, Britain's archaic Whitworth fasteners? No, phew; some judicious paint-scraping from one new wrench and I was back in business.

But frustration aside, what a rush to be grasping, turning, touching, working with my hands! Even if the work had to be redone; even if it seemed slow at times, staccato, fruitless. The shine on a polished bearing race; the heft of a half-axle; the chill from a brake assembly picked up early on a winter morning. You couldn't appreciate the feeling, the parts, unless you did it yourself—and God knows you wouldn't while working on an assembly line; perhaps especially on an assembly line, where you hardly had a free moment to express admiration. Did Chapman realize the Seven defied as well as followed Henry Ford? That his impractical Seven would become, paradoxically, a latter-day Model T, one of the few cars an owner was expected to maintain himself?

There was an elegance in the Seven's suspension that spoke of simpler, more thoughtful times. You could see how Chapman made one part do the work of two or three, found graceful solutions to complicated mechanical dilemmas. The front wheels need to be positioned, damped, and stabilized at the same time: Was there a way to combine those requirements in a single assembly? Yes, if you're Chapman: connect most everything through the damper unit, from springs to antiroll bar.

Chapman was an adept student of William of Occam—the man behind Occam's Razor, the idea and ideal that "entities should not be multiplied unnecessarily." (Occam, were he alive today, might run a consulting firm with the motto "Keep it simple, stupid.") Progress, here, was measured by elimination rather than addition, telling the builder that complicated questions could yield surprisingly simple answers.

The front suspension on my Seven is quite different from the 1957 original. From ten feet away, however, few people could tell the difference, which demonstrates the classic nature of Chapman's design. Caterham's fidelity has been deliberate, mostly to retain the Seven's distinctive look, but also because it allowed an enormous amount of fine-tuning. Chapman, by contrast, left the Seven alone for purely practical reasons. He threatened to fire anyone who suggested updates or improvements, according to Arnold, because he saw little reason to invest in an aging design; changes were made only "if a supplier refused to deliver due to nonpayment, or if a major component went out of production." Chapman was too miserly—or too sentimental, perhaps—to alter the car until it was absolutely necessary.

You can see Chapman's point. Why ruin a good thing? The Seven's design has stood the test of time: Its tubular steel space frame, more or less full-body roll cage (produced for both Lotus and Caterham by Arch Motors), makes the car solid and steady, and its riveted aluminum panels give the chassis a rigidity that Detroit engineers have achieved only recently. Figure out just the right place to add reliable components—a five-speed manual transmission, disc brakes for every wheel, rack-and-pinion steering, independent suspension, antiroll bars front and rear—and you've got a car that's responsive, efficient, and quick. And easy to maintain, too: Although Caterham increasingly uses proprietary components, many replacement parts can be purchased at local car dealers or auto-supply stores.

My Seven is full of Ford items—the engine, the transmission, the hubs, the constant velocity joints (the universal joints between the half-shafts and the wheels). And that's appropriate, for the Seven's assembly isn't so different from the Model T's nearly a century ago; it's an eccentric example of ontogeny recapitulating phylogeny. Like Chapman, Henry

Ford began as an assembler of cars, not a manufacturer; the Model T's chassis, engine, and axles were supplied by the Dodge Brothers, for example, the bodies by a local coachmaker. Ford saw no reason, like Chapman after him, to reinvent a component when an existing one could be modified or adapted to a new purpose.

Ford and Chapman also shared a belief in mechanical efficiency. Of the many twice-told tales about Chapman, perhaps the most famous is his testing prototypes on the track and then removing chassis tubes until the frame collapsed . . . whereupon he put the last-removed tube back in. Ford said pretty much the same thing in his autobiography, writing that car making should be based not on "cheapening of the manufacturing"—the standard approach, he claimed—but in "eliminating the entirely useless parts." Ford was an Occamite, too.

Although Ford made his name as a mass producer, and Chapman as an exotic specialist, there are even parallels between them in the auto-racing world. Ford realized, well before designing the Model T, that the best way—possibly the only way—to improve his car and business prospects was to gain publicity through racing. In 1901 he entered, and won, his first competition, and the following year set a world speed record (though as a maker, not a driver; by then the man behind the wheel was famed bicycle racer Barney Oldfield, who had learned to drive only a week earlier). Ford won these contests mainly because his cars were much lighter than his competitors', just as Lotus would win races because its cars were lighter than Enzo Ferrari's.

The Seven tips the scales at under 1,300 pounds, about half the weight of a modern Honda Accord. It doesn't take a very big engine, consequently, to get the car to cruising speed and beyond, nor huge, heavy brakes to get it to stop. Pure speed, though, isn't the point. The Seven gives the driver, above all, the sense of being at one with the road, as if it were an extension of the driver's body. As more than one automotive writer has commented, you don't get into a Seven so much as put it on. Maybe that's why the Seven, at bottom, looks less like a production car than a fashion designer's fantasy. If Erte had been asked to draw his dream car, this might have been the result.

My dream car in 1972 was a big, white, powerful Buick LeSabre with a wide bench seat perfect for drive-ins. So what if it was nine years old, had a cracked block, drove (as John noted) like a sofa? It was a car, I was sixteen, and this was California; without one I was, well, nothing.

When you spend your teenage years in the suburbs, ten miles from downtown and twenty miles from school, the yearning for car ownership is visceral. There's the backseat, of course, for those lovingly imagined trysts, but the need runs deeper. When you've arranged to meet up with car-owning friends, it's profoundly embarrassing to arrive by bike or—worst of all—be dropped off by your mother. I couldn't understand it: Why would my parents trade in the Buick at a ridiculously low price when I'd be thrilled to take possession—not paying top dollar, perhaps, but at least family dollars. I begged, I cajoled, I complained that many classmates had cars: Mustangs, Capris, Chevys, old Fords, ancient Volvos, almost-new BMWs, even an International Harvester pickup truck.

My parents said *no*.

I don't recall how I reacted, exactly, but chances are I adopted the morose teenager act. Late to dinner, early to leave, monosyllabic answers, refusing to look relatives in the eye, and generally laying on the guilt as thickly as possible. And you know what? It worked, for a few days later my father said he and Mom were reconsidering. It was quite a moment—not least because I, too, was reconsidering, having realized the Buick was probably, and almost literally, a white elephant.

If I took title I'd most likely have to get a new engine, and worry about insurance and registration and emission systems ... and why bother, since I could probably borrow Mom's new, beige Audi most anytime? (Only years later did it become clear—Mom still refuses to acknowledge the truth—that the 100LS model was a Grade A lemon.) My parents rarely went out nights and weekends, and separately, almost never; at least one car was usually in the garage, and I had no reason to think it would be off-limits. My desire for a pink slip became vanishingly small, in short, when the mooching prospects loomed large.

My brief fling with the Buick encapsulates pretty well the typical love/hate relationship with automobiles. Fantasies of speed and thrills, domination and independence, evolve into a hazy nightmare of breakdowns and recalls, worries and bills. The gap between perception and reality, small at first, widens dramatically as cars and their owners age; when you're young and unseasoned, all you care about is image, believing reality can be made from the outside in. Hence the common lust—at my school, at least—for Vicky's red, four-on-the-floor BMW 2002, for Robbie's hunter green, wide-tired 1965 Mustang (with Holley carbs and headers under the hood, if I remember correctly). Those were truly sexy cars ... unlike, say, the silver Chevelle driven by my best pal, Hugh, or the transportation I often borrowed, my father's Plymouth Valiant. Hugh and I comforted ourselves with half-fond, half-mocking nicknames: The Chevy became The Sexmobile, and the Valiant—bright yellow outside, mustard yellow inside, much like a certain coastal invertebrate—The Slugmobile.

In Santa Barbara we adolescents lived a minor version, fifteen years down the road, of *American Graffiti*. No elusive blondes in white Thunderbirds, certainly, or deadly midnight road races, but the same overriding concerns: sex and sub-stance abuse. And it was automobiles that made the search for those unholy grails not merely convenient but possible. Cruising State Street on Saturday night, halfheartedly look-ing for (human) pickups; taking a girlfriend into the back-country to see the spring wildflowers and possibly some naked flesh (hers); convening at Gary's parents' house most weekends, in the detached cottage dubbed The Cave, and lis-tening to Pink Floyd, Monty Python, John Prine, the Grate-ful Dead. One night, driving home under the influence of some particularly strong marijuana, I straddled for miles the double yellow line on East Valley Road, convinced I was on the Dead's Golden Road to Unlimited Devotion.

And those trips to Los Angeles. To see James Earl Jones in *Othello*, in a vehicle thoughtfully equipped with a portable bar; the adults (not mine) drank so much en route I wondered if we'd get home alive. By bus to Disneyland for Grad Night, when the park was open from midnight to dawn for high-school seniors and their guests: I'd wager that at least a third of the visitors that night were high (we Cave people cooked up Toklas brownies for consumption en route). And most memorably, the school trip for an event at the Dorothy Chan-dler Pavilion, to which I was allowed, for some reason, to chauffeur my first serious girlfriend. I can't remember the name of the play; I can't forget the aftermath, for an hour or two of steamy backseat good-byes concluded with my locking myself out of the Audi right in Dina's driveway. She volun-teered to drive me home, a thirty-mile round-trip, to retrieve a spare key, but I opted—it being four in the morning on a school night—to break a rear quarter window instead. Replacing it cost something like $30, which seemed a fortune at the time, and Dina never let me forget that I alone skipped school the following day.

Cars play such a major role in California high-school life

that it's surprising to recall how little they influenced my college years. True, we road-tripped to women's schools once or twice, but Yale had recently gone co-ed, and the train station was within walking distance of campus. I had a car nonetheless, for John was living in Manhattan then and preferred loaning me his Datsun 510 wagon—formerly owned by my brother David and the twin of the car I would buy the following year—to parking it in New York. I learned to work a manual transmission in this car, thanks to my roommate Paul, and to the annoyance of the school in whose empty parking lot we practiced. Officials shooed us away, despite knowing full well what we were up to—the constantly bucking car, with occasional roaring starts and sudden, dieseling stops, was unmistakable evidence of a stick-shift novice's thrashings.

My purpose in buying my own 510 that postfreshman summer was purely utilitarian: for the annual migrations between California and Connecticut. It did the job: Purchased in Santa Barbara with 55,000 miles on the odometer, the car was alive years later at 105,000 (at which point I passed it on to Morris, another roommate still languishing in New Haven). In my twenties by this time, I wanted a nonstudent car and found myself hankering for the new Mazda 626 coupe, which the auto magazines had hailed as a "Japanese BMW." That was a good description, at least when compared to the Datsun: The five-speed transmission was slick, the handling direct, the tires wide and gripping. I put over 100,000 miles on the Mazda, and would have added many more had it not been stolen during my tenth college reunion. By then I was living in New York City, so the crime—considering the thousands of dollars I spent annually on parking and insurance—actually came as a relief. My one regret is having dropped theft insurance weeks before the car disappeared.

Perhaps you can read lives in auto-biographical terms. Buick sedan, Datsun wagon, Mazda coupe; between 1972 and

1988, the cars I coveted got smaller, sportier, sexier. To make the auto arc unmistakable, though, I should note one other car, owned concurrently with the 626: a 1963, navy blue Lancia Flaminia coupe with leather interior, three carburetors, an oil cooler, and a wood-trimmed steering wheel. I didn't need the car, which I bought for $5,500 from the estate of my father's oldest friend: I just wanted it, because I had a good, career-starting job at a magazine and because the Lancia was so odd, so alluring, so stylish. The purchase was a mistake, of course, as I had neither the time nor the skill to care for an elderly, eccentric automobile. It was a sign of things to come, however, and I regret selling the Lancia, at a large loss, to an Italian-car lover who promised to restore the Lancia to its former glory. I hope he did.

My experience with the Lancia should have put me off exotic sports cars. But it didn't, of course, for that's not how things work with automobiles, or any fixation: I learned not *Never fall in love with the unknown* but *Don't fight the feeling.* (Human romance, of course, follows the same treacherous path.) The Seven would sit at the apex of my car adventures, and go some way toward rendering the others coherent.

4

THE ROAD TO DETROIT

Once I noticed the links between Chapman and Ford, the Seven and the Model T, it was difficult to keep myself out of bookstores. That was my natural environment; my first published article in adulthood was a book review, and over the last two decades I've written more book criticism than anything else. Building the Seven was frighteningly out of character, and the best way to make the project unfrightening, I reckoned, was to anchor myself with information.

The volumes shelved in "Automobile" sections were usually disappointing. They showed a clear left-brain/right-brain bifurcation; there were celebrations (*man, look at the size of that turbocharger!*) and excoriations (*cars, they've destroyed communities left and right*), with the middle ground occupied only by utilitarian books, how-tos and how-not-to-get-ripped-offs. Passion, pro and con, ruled the car-book aisles; the automobile plays such an enormous role in our lives that no one, apparently, could perceive it whole, or with disinterest.

The books I ended up reading were biographies and memoirs, academic histories and industrial chronicles, political analyses and personal commentaries. They told me, together, that the automobile has shaped world culture more than any other invention by becoming the planet's biggest manufacturing industry, inaugurating automated mass production, using up most of the earth's energy resources, specializing labor to an unimaginable degree, fostering suburbia and class difference. And the more I read, the stranger it seemed that most people drive these large, expensive, dangerous, decisive machines with little knowledge of their workings. We buy cars to feel powerful, independent, desirable, in control, but in truth we put ourselves at the mercy of untold designers and mechanics and politicians and businessmen. One could say, adapting Henry David Thoreau for modern times, that we don't ride upon cars; they ride upon us.

Henry Ford will always be remembered, and ridiculed, for saying "History is more or less bunk." And that's unfortunate, because his basic point was reasonable, equivalent to Stephen Dedalus calling history—almost contemporaneously—"a nightmare from which I am trying to awake." Ford, speaking during World War I, believed that memories of bloodshed and old slights were responsible for most warfare and worry, and consequently that "the only history that is worth a tinker's damn is the history we make today." Real history, to Ford, was the story of progress, of tools, because "our country had depended more on harrows than on guns and speeches. I thought that history which excluded harrows, and all the rest of daily life, was bunk. And I think so yet."

Ford would be pleased that social and technological history, today, are major academic fields. More—that some scholars consider the history of the modern West to be the same, at bottom, as the history of technology, for what seminal event in the twentieth century wasn't predicated on machine-generated power? In the United States alone, the Wright brothers' flight at Kitty Hawk, the bombing of Hiroshima and Nagasaki, the landing on the moon, the pervasive use of electricity; none would have occurred without fuel-powered engines. And neither could, of course, the motor car, the most profound phenomenon of them all.

For centuries the idea of a self-propelled vehicle was pure fantasy. But people did think about it; Roger Bacon wrote in the thirteenth century that "cars can be made so that without animals they will move with unbelievable rapidity," and Leonardo da Vinci, three hundred years later, drew a vehicle resembling a modern tank. The wind, for a time, seemed the likeliest source of power; an Italian physician in 1335 drew plans for a military wagon propelled by a roof-mounted windmill. By the mid-seventeenth century, however, steam showed promise, with two Jesuit missionaries in China apparently the first to develop a self-propelled, steam-powered carriage. But that experiment had no progeny; another century passed before Nicholas Cugnot, in 1769, used steam to drive the three-wheeled vehicle that many consider the first automobile. This ungainly contraption moved only as fast as a man could walk and left the road on encountering its first turn, yet demonstrated convincingly that motorized transport was possible.

Steam power was the order of the day. Widely used in ore-mine drainage pumps in the early 1700s, steam engines grew more and more efficient and practical as Thomas Newcomen, James Watt, and Matthew Boulton improved on the pioneering work of Thomas Savery. By the end of the century high-pressure boilers had been designed, paving the way for the first commercially plausible self-powered transport. In 1801 English mining engineer Richard Trevithick (who died in

Dartford, Kent, home to the Caterham works) built a steam-powered carriage, and in 1804 the first steam-powered railway locomotive. In 1805 Oliver Evans produced for Philadelphia a self-propelled, ground- and water-going dredge (bearing the wonderful name "Orukter Amphibolos," or "Amphibious Digger"); in 1807 Robert Fulton ran his first steamboat up the Hudson. By 1832, a steam-powered bus was making regular runs between central London and Paddington.

Britain, being the birthplace of the Industrial Revolution, had every reason to lead the world in small, road-engine technology. And it did, for a time ... until the thriving railroad industry—Trevithick's heirs—pressured Parliament to authorize the Red Flag Act of 1865, which limited road vehicles to speeds of four miles per hour. With the incentive to develop better engines in England thus crippled, France and the United States took up the slack. In the mid-1880s Count Albert de Dion, with his partner Georges Bouton, built steam tricycles outside Paris, and a few years later Ransom Olds did the same in Michigan. The following decade saw the invention of the Stanley Steamer and the Locomobile steamer, the latter becoming, in 1900–1901, the best-selling automobile in the United States.

But steam power turned out to be a dead end, at least for road-going vehicles. Steam engines were heavy, inefficient, slow to start, and dangerous: There had to be a better way. Electrical engines? Tens of thousand of electric cars would be produced by 1900, and many more thereafter, but all suffered from the flaw that hinders their development today; limited range, due to the short life of battery charges. Gasoline engines? That was indeed the future, as some recognized following Nicolas Otto's 1876 creation, in Germany, of the four-cycle engine. The Otto engine initially ran on coal gas; in 1885 former Otto employee Gottlieb Daimler modified it to burn gasoline, and so produced the first high-speed internal-combustion engine. That same year Daimler and his assistant Wilhelm Maybach—who would go on to invent, in 1892, the modern carburetor—produced a motorcycle using the improved Otto engine.

Paternity for the modern automobile, despite the foregoing, is usually attributed to Karl Benz, mainly because he demonstrated the auto's commercial viability. (It didn't hurt that his vehicle acted more like a modern car than Daimler's, having three wheels rather than two and starting by way of a spark plug rather than a hot tube.) Benz, at first using a simple two-cycle engine, sold barely a dozen vehicles between 1885 and 1892. He was more committed to the automobile than many other carmakers, however, and would sell hundreds of vehicles annually (now with four wheels) by the turn of the century. Benz's first four-wheeler was built in 1893, the same year the Duryea brothers produced America's first successful gas-powered car; they were inspired by a description of Benz's three-wheeler in an 1889 *Scientific American*.

For years Benz sold most of his cars in France, then the capital of the embryonic automobile industry. In 1901 more than 130 carmakers were based in greater Paris, one result of France's having the world's best roads. France, not coincidentally, also boasted a thriving bicycle industry—the velocipede was invented in Paris in the 1860s—led by Armand Peugeot, who realized that the wealthy would prefer motorized four-wheelers to self-propelled two-wheelers. In subsequent years car buyers were limited, according to one French study, to "wealthy sportsmen, doctors, businessmen, and engineers"—in other words, to the rich, the curious, and the peripatetic.

The chief engineer, at the time, of Detroit's main Edison power plant had only contempt for such people (engineers aside). His name was Henry Ford, and before long he would put his contempt to good use; he would build a car "for the great multitude." Ford wasn't the first to articulate that vision—Olds and the Duryeas shared it independently—but Ford's "better idea" came to life with unparalleled success.

Ford was by birth a plainspoken country boy, but a contradictory one. He loved the idea of farms but hated the long, hard, repetitive labor they entailed; he disliked books, but when he did read popular works was likely to pick up something by Thoreau or Ralph Waldo Emerson. (A game-room mantel in his Dearborn estate bore Thoreau's advice to "Chop your own wood and it will warm you twice.") Ford once gave a car to technophobic nature writer John Burroughs so he could "know nature better," and the gift provides another insight into Ford's genius. Not many people, even then, saw noisy, smelly automobiles as compatible with wild, green nature, but Ford's understanding of such incongruities laid the foundations for his business.

As with the automobile itself, Ford's major problem was getting his company started. Only wealthy people bought cars; how could you make money selling automobiles, let alone quality automobiles, to average Joes? It was these and similar issues—and Ford's naturally autocratic personality—that led to the demise of Ford's first two car ventures, the Detroit Automobile Company (formed 1899) and the Henry Ford Company (formed 1901). Ford's insistence on building a sturdy, well-engineered car clashed directly with his investors' hopes for quick profits.

You might think, after these early failures, that Ford would treat his third set of backers with kid gloves. But no: When Ford's partner in his next carmaking attempt, the Ford Motor Company (formed 1903), suggested focusing on upscale, high-margin touring cars, Ford refused to go along. He clung steadfastly to an insight eluding better-educated, more sophisticated money men; that the average worker was "more a buyer than a seller." By designing a car that was inexpensive to build, buy, and maintain, Ford could square the capitalist circle: make the automobile producer, and the automobile consumer, one and the same.

The Ford Motor Company, keeping to its founder's vision, triumphed almost instantly. Ford paid off his initial investors within the year, and by 1906—the same year he introduced the Model N and started writing himself into the history books— had bought out his remaining partner. The N was described by a contemporaneous automobile trade magazine as "distinctly the most important mechanical traction event of 1906," but of much greater moment was the efficiency with which the car was built. "I believe that I have solved the problem of cheap as well as simple automobile construction," Ford told the press. He wasn't exaggerating: Within a few months Ford was able to deliver one hundred Model Ns in a single day.

It was the Model T, of course, that made Ford an industrial titan. Between 1908 and 1927 over fifteen million were built, and no car would sell more until the Volkswagen Beetle; in 1920, every other car on the planet was a T. The model's greatest historical significance lay not in its popularity or mechanics, however, but its production methods. Ford loved craft and craftsmen, for the freedom and self-reliance they represented, and loved cars for the same reasons . . . yet ended up sacrificed one to the other, doing to craftsmen what he also did, unwittingly, to farmers—set loose a force that made their world obsolete. In his old age Ford would devote much time to building Greenfield Village, a faux historic town in Dearborn celebrating handicrafts and mechanical arts, and it's difficult to avoid viewing the re-creation as anything but an apology for the simple, rural, self-sufficient life that Ford, more than anyone else, was responsible for destroying.

The major cause of that destruction was the assembly line. Ford didn't invent it—grain mills and meatpackers had long used continuous-flow systems, though more often for disassembly than assembly—but came close to perfecting the idea. Ford's future head of production, Charles Sorenson, created a primitive moving assembly line in 1908 by loading a Model N chassis on skids and dragging it past component-assembly areas; Ford encouraged Sorenson to refine the process, and by 1913 moving assembly lines had become the centerpiece of the company's new, sixty-two-acre Highland Park plant. The assembly lines (for which Sorenson got little credit, to his lifelong chagrin) were astonishing, usually dependable, extremely effective, and fatal to the tradesman's way of life.

Who needs skilled tradesmen when their skills could be built into machines, machines more precise than men and that rarely wearied, never walked out? Which could be manned by low-paid laborers, themselves easily replaced if they became, for whatever reason, balky, inefficient, troublesome? Assembly lines still required some skilled tradesmen, such as the tool-and-die makers who created the line machines, but once up and running, the system required little but brawn and animal stamina.

This was true "mass production"—a term first published in the 1926 *Encyclopedia Britannica* in an article of the same name bearing Henry Ford's byline. Ignorance, not talent, was the characteristic Ford sought in workers, since uneducated and unskilled employees were more likely to tolerate the mind-numbing routine of assembly-line manufacturing. That's one reason Ford was willing to take a chance on almost anyone "whether he has been in Sing Sing or at Harvard," as Ford put it, so long as he (and eventually, she) showed "the desire to work."

Much ink has been spilled on the destructive side effects of automating labor. Thoreau was among the first to note the inversion of mechanic and mechanism, writing in *Walden* that "men have become the tools of their tools." (Did Ford encounter that passage? If so, one wonders how he responded.) Karl Marx, born a year after Thoreau, in 1818, was overtly political in his analysis, which he began formulating about the time Thoreau retreated to Walden Pond but stated most concisely decades later, in *Das Kapital*. "In handi-crafts and manufacture," he wrote, "the workman makes use of a tool; in the factory, the machine makes use of him." Marx, dying in 1883, probably never saw an automobile—let alone an automobile factory—but there's little doubt his con-cept of the alienation of labor, hinted at in the quotation above, found its apotheosis on the automobile assembly line.

Listen to the following description of life in such a plant in 1934. "[I]n order to 'make the grade,'" wrote one assembly-line laborer,

> one has to repeat movement after movement faster than one can think, so that not only reflection but even day-dreaming is impossible. In front of his machine, the worker has to annihilate his soul, his thought, his feelings, everything, for eight hours a day.

The worker? Simone Weil, on the line at a Renault assembly plant.

That should come as a surprise, for Weil is remembered today as a mystical, idiosyncratic religious philosopher. But in her youth—in truth, she was always young, dying at thirty-four in an English sanitarium a short drive from Caterham Cars—she was obsessed with manual labor, mainly because it was so foreign to her bookish, intellectual nature. At first Weil regarded working with her hands as an "escape . . . from a world of abstractions," but by the time this eight-month "escape" was over she saw factory work as a kind of slavery. Weil left Renault suffering from eczema, dizziness, headaches, nervous exhaustion, and the sense that she was scarcely human, deserving no better treatment than a barn cat or junkyard dog.

Weil ran a milling machine—on which, one day, she ground off part of a thumb—at a factory in a Paris suburb. She chose the Billancourt plant for good reason; twenty years earlier it had been the site of a famous strike against a new work method that complemented Ford's mass-production techniques. Ford sought efficiency in assembly methods and machines; Frederick Winslow Taylor, seven years Ford's senior, chased efficiency in the workers themselves. Taylorism and Fordism for many years functioned well together, but the former, in its pure iteration, fell by the wayside much sooner—in part because Taylor, unlike Ford, disdained the ordinary working stiff. Taylor once wore a blue collar himself, but forgot his roots after becoming a world-renowned expositor of "scientific management."

Taylor initially made a name for himself as an engineer, developing in the 1890s superior metal cutters for lathes (the first mass-production machine, coincidentally) while employed by Bethlehem Steel. The high-speed blades were demonstrated at the Paris Exposition of 1900, after which the "Taylor process" became famous and its inventor, rich. Rich, too, is the irony, for the steel company's exhibit was installed only a few hundred yards from the electric "dynamo" that made Henry Adams, in *The Education of Henry Adams*, quail as if before a new God. Adams's fears about modern technology, the "irruption of forces totally new," were even better exemplified by the work of F. W. Taylor, for Taylor had no intention of limiting himself to the improvement of machines. He had bigger fish to fry; he also wanted to upgrade the men who operated the machines, and even men independently of machines.

Taylor, in search of unprecedented industrial productivity, envisioned a bifurcated working world in which managers contributed thought and workers only sweat. In this neo-social-Darwinian view, executives created and ran a system that the workers implemented, their every move prescribed in detail by their presumed betters. Why the hard-and-fast split? Because the worker "resembles in his mental make-up the ox"; so wrote Taylor in his seminal (and racist) *The Principles of Scientific Management*, published in 1911. Taylor, who was appalled at any shop "really run by the workers," believed that employees labored efficiently only when toeing a management-made line.

Taylorism was predicated on the idea that "every single act of every workman can be reduced to a science," which meant sending clipboard-bearing, stopwatch-thumbing managers onto work sites and shop floors to uncover the "one best way" of performing everyday tasks. (The authoritarian nature of the endeavor is best expressed, perhaps, by Taylorism's being embraced by both Lenin and Mussolini.) And the automobile industry loved such time-and-motion studies, especially in Europe, not only because they "rationalized" manufacturing but because they rejected the craftsman ethic; Taylorism was, in essence, an early form of union busting. Its originator claimed to have the workers' best interests at heart, since those who accepted Taylorization earned higher wages, but for thousands it meant unemployment, debilitating stress, and disdain toward once-valued skills.

In most quarters, today, Taylorism is considered quaint, an historical artifact that deserved its early death. In truth, though, Taylorism didn't die so much as change its clothes and blend in. And it did so, oddly enough, partly through humorous literature—mainly *Cheaper by the Dozen*, the 1949 best-seller (and later, film) in which two children of Frank and Lillian Gilbreth, Taylor allies who pioneered time-and-motion studies, recount their father's attempts to apply scientific management on the home front. Frank Gilbreth tried to shave simultaneously with two straight razors; insisted his twelve children listen to language-instruction records while bathing; taught them Morse code by painting the cipher alphabet on the walls of their Nantucket vacation home. This was Taylorism watered down until it became amusing, unthreatening—even though the father, who made every family rule and often exempted himself from same, declared the Gilbreth clan a democracy.

Modified, and often under the rubric "work studies,"

time-and-motion techniques are still in use today. Indeed, they helped push me out of my last full-time job, as a reporter and editor at the State Bar of California's legal magazine. The bar was a politically divided and disliked organization, so the executives did what executives frequently do under similar circumstances: They hired a consultant. The consulting firm, knowing who paid the bills, ferreted out numerous problems, few of them traceable (surprise!) to administrative practice. I was asked to fill out forms; to describe a typical workday; to submit to subtle surveillance. I wasn't, so far as I know, timed.

I remain unclear how the information so gleaned was supposed to make me more efficient and productive—would it help me charm sources into speaking freely? Think through a chain of causation? Settle on just the right description? Unquestionably, though, the experience made me pessimistic about organized work. I told a friend, who happened to be a management consultant, about the experience, and he passed on the old business-school joke. *Consultant: someone who borrows your watch in order to tell you the time.*

But the most significant effects of Taylorism are nothing to joke about. It embedded in work culture the notion that worker efficiency, and by extension the bottom line, are the prime goal of business, and that the division between worker and manager should be decisive. What's more, Taylor's core belief—"In the past the man has been first; in the future the system must be first"—still holds, as may be judged from the fact that the uber-manager himself, Peter Drucker, has called Taylorism "the most powerful as well as the most lasting contribution America has made to Western thought since the Federalist papers." Drucker considers Taylor, not Marx, the third member of the trinity (the others are Darwin and Freud) that shaped the modern world.

Men, post-Taylor, really were tools of their tools, and not just metaphorically.

5

THE MECHANICAL MIND

I first laid eyes on a Seven in the summer of 1975, when I worked with Les at a bicycle shop in London's refurbished Covent Garden. I had just finished my freshman year of college, and those weeks represented a wonderful respite from the rigors, and luxury, of academics. Not least because of my lodgings: Les lived in a Raskolnikovian garret in a nineteenth-century rowhouse on the edge of Bloomsbury, and I rented a dank room on the second floor that contained a straw mattress so worn you couldn't roll out of bed if you tried. Les paid something like £2½ a week, I paid £5, and we got our money's worth . . . barely.

Les was a fixture in my adolescent life, and one reason was his refusal to go along with what used to be called "late capitalism." He had no interest in political theory, least of all Marxist thought, yet lived more like a true-believing socialist than anyone you can name. He might have been a native Santa Barbarian—locals prefer to drop the *1*, of course—but his home was a burnt-out adobe hacienda furnished almost exclusively with recycled and salvaged goods. He survived on vegetarian, often home-grown fare, and traveled by bicycle or, infrequently, clapped-out car. I first read *Walden* the year I met Les, and although I didn't understand the book at the time, even a naive sixteen-year-old could tell he was a latter-day Thoreau. He certainly followed one bit of Thoreauvian advice: "Beware of all enterprises that require new clothes."

Les's homestead broke every building code in the book. It had once been a dream house, a Spanish-style villa on double-digit acres with a pool, an olive grove, and a spectacular view of the Pacific. Built in a then-secluded canyon, the house burned almost to the ground in a wildfire months after his family moved in. It was a total loss . . . except to Les, who began to fix up the place while completing his doctoral studies. He reroofed the kitchen, a bathroom, and the dining room—adobe walls withstood the fire—and for the next few years lived a pauper's life with a princely vista.

Les, needless to say, was—is—eccentric, and I suppose my high school should be commended for hiring him at all. Or maybe not, since Latin teachers always seem a mite odd. (The school's previous instructor—mother to a mortician—gave us "Latin pills" over vacation, vocabulary words rolled up in half-inch lengths of soda straw; her predecessor was an enigmatic bachelor who drowned himself, rocks-in-the-pockets like Virginia Woolf, in a lake.) Les's contract wasn't extended, in any case, for a second year, and a major reason was his fraternization with students. He was too friendly, too strange, too undignified; no doubt some parent complained after hearing (for example) that Les had allowed Sarah H. to draw psychedelic spirals on his eyeglasses. Students, of course, found such informality and antiauthoritarianism in a teacher quite refreshing. Les might not be cool, but he was consistently nonconformist and thus someone even disaffected, supercilious teenagers could look up to.

After Les was fired, Hugh and I developed a Friday ritual. We'd meet Les somewhere—at his parents' new house, a friend's place, at the university, wherever Les happened to be studying or odd-jobbing or repairing somebody's car—stick his bike in the trunk, and head to a cheap local grocery. Les would buy a quart of Rainier Ale—he was partial to The Green Death—and Hugh or I would buy the cheese. Then we'd drive into the hills: past the mission, past the natural history museum, past the botanical garden, up and up until we hit Les's driveway, paved for the first hundred yards but subsequently, after the gate, dirt and weeds and gravel. The half-mile hike to the house was always exhilarating: the dazzling panorama, the sage- and chaparral scented air, the quail skittering and the vultures wheeling, the prospect of good food, effective beer, and chaotic, animated, subversive conversation.

Les usually made dinner—pizza and cabbage salad, as a rule, sausage pizza if we could overcome Les's growing vegetarian scruples—because, like most everything he attempted, he was good at it. Classical music, or Paul Robeson's "Songs of My People," played on the stereo, Les's one concession to consumer culture; the rest of the house looked like a packrat's den. The kitchen chairs had lumber scraps where the rattan used to be, the backseat of Les's Peugeot doubled as the sofa; the sink (cold water only) and toilet worked, but with the nearest discernible house miles away, we generally peed outside, just because. To wash up after vegetable planting or olive-oil pressing or brush cutting or cement mixing, you'd use a garden hose, though in extreme circumstances visitors climbed into the bathtub (on the roof, for solar heating).

Those sojourns in Mission Canyon were our 1920s Paris, our improvised bohemia, the perfect antidote to the languid serenity that made Santa Barbara attractive to everyone besides congenitally discontented teenagers.

By the time I caught up with Les in London, years later, he had stripped his life even further. The landlady, then in her seventies, didn't exactly discourage frugal ways; a childless widow, the quite wonderful Mrs. Forsythe had very little money (in part because she charged such low rents) and didn't mind Les's cutting up old telephone books for toilet paper or filling the tenants' kitchen with dumpster-retrieved paraphernalia. His diet was now limited to expired cheese, vegetables scavenged from the farmer's market, pinto beans bought in twenty-five-kilo bags (transported home, somehow, by bike), whole-wheat waffles, home-roasted peanuts, and bread baked in the coin-operated stove (5p for ten minutes of gas, if memory serves). Squatters living in the numerous condemned buildings nearby may have spent fewer pence per annum than Les, but I doubt it.

Les pointed out a Seven one afternoon as we were returning from free showers at the University of London gym. The car was yellow and thoroughly dwarfed by the others surrounding it; they looked ready to pounce, held back only by the Seven's pugnacious, buggy expression. Les said the owner lived a block or two away, and sure enough, a few days later we saw him get in the car and drive off. He could have picked up loose change in the road, I noticed, without undoing his seat belt.

Les told me a little of the car's history, and said it'd be fun to build one together someday. The idea wasn't utterly far-fetched; I was helping Les assemble bicycles at the bike shop, we'd once put together a stereo amplifier (there's a Dynaco amp somewhere with a label inside saying, in Latin, "Les and Chris made me"), and I'd already made plans to construct a

Heathkit television. My experience with kits, on the other hand, wasn't totally positive. Everything I built worked in the end, and for a good long while, but I never learned as much as I expected to. I became adept at following directions, checking off to-do boxes, soldering transistors and resistors and capacitors . . . yet when I flipped the switch and the lights began to glow, I understood electricity no better than when the kit landed on my doorstep.

A car kit, of course, was a quantum leap upward, and I wouldn't have considered tackling it without Les. But I also knew he frequently suggested projects that never came to fruition, largely because everyone we knew was too busy studying, or engaged in a livelihood, or raising a family, to get them off the ground. On the car front alone, Les and I had talked about modifying prewar, front-wheel-drive Citroëns— they looked perfect for a 1930s Chicago gangster movie—to export stateside, and refurbishing the 1950s Jaguar falling apart in Les's parents' garage.

But Les's proposals were fantasies in any case, lovely pipe dreams. Besides, I had a career to build; how could I justify building a car just for the love, the thrill of it? Automobiles, what's more, were no particular passion of mine, and of decreasing interest to Les; since moving to England he'd hardly driven one. For all that, though, the idea of building a Seven was always in the back of my mind—and returned full-force in 1978, when San Francisco's public-television station broadcast *The Prisoner* in its entirety. By then a graduate student in journalism at UC Berkeley, I became a member of KQED just to get the promotional T-shirt, on which Number Six says "I'm THE PRISONER of Channel Nine." The shirt's a little ragged now, but I still have it.

Fifteen years would pass between that first encounter with the Seven and my irrevocable decision to build one. Much had changed in the interim—particularly me, for I had realized by then that my professional life might encompass such a project. The jobs I had held, the training endured in journalism and law, had heightened my understanding of the chasms between work cultures; had demonstrated that experience in a particular line of work often led people to devalue other kinds—to misinterpret, often willfully, others' ways of knowing.

Would building a Seven provide insight into the meaning of work? Its significance? Help me understand why workers in different fields, or on different levels in the same field, developed disparate worldviews? Allow me to comprehend why people like Les and Thoreau and Weil, despite myriad talents, had trouble finding a comfortable place in the world? That was the central dilemma in Thoreau's life, after all, what drove him to Walden: the quest to "respire and aspire both at once" (as one scholar put it). Building a Seven would be unlike any other task I had undertaken . . . and sufficiently different, perhaps, to force me to see familiar things in new ways, and old things previously overlooked.

Assembly of the suspension took only a few hours, but in the course of it I reached, much sooner than anticipated, the point of no return. The joints between the dampers and the lower wishbones had to be "Loctited."

Loctite is probably the most familiar brand of "anaerobic threadlocker," a liquid sealant that cures in the absence of air and ensures that what's been done will not be undone. Loctite comes in a number of varieties; Red Loctite 271, the kind I used, is intended (according to the package) for the assembly of "critical fasteners such as rocker arms, differentials and bottom ends of piston rods." Loctite creates a secure joint because it fastens bolt threads within the bolt hole, thus reducing vibration, while simultaneously preventing the entry of contaminants like dirt and water. That's well and good—

but once Loctite has cured, you may have to heat a joint to 450 degrees to take it apart. Just what I needed: the chance to make a mistake remedied not with a wrench but a blowtorch.

Holding my breath, and after reading the relevant section of the assembly manual for the umpteenth time, I Loctited the wishbone/damper joints. I also Loctited the studs on each end of the front antiroll bar, which fit (by way of internally threaded balls) into the upper wishbone and transform the front suspension into a single, roll-resistant unit. (Lateral roll, that is: You want the car to roll backwards and forwards, but not sideways.) Here, though, I may have made a mistake, for it was difficult to identify the moment at which the antiroll-bar studs bottomed out. On this point the manual, as often proved the case, was silent: It hadn't been updated to reflect a minor change in the bar's design, and made no reference to depth of stud penetration.

Under different circumstances I might have wiped off the Loctite and called a responsible someone for advice. But to phone Chris on my second day of assembly? To hear him say, in his dashing-but-authoritative accent, "You didn't really, did you?" For a problem that I should be able, novice or not, to figure out myself? No way.

Solomon-like, I mentally divided each stud in half; assigned one half to the antiroll bar and one half to the threaded ball; Loctited them; and installed the entire assembly. It fit like a charm, and works fine to this day. As far as I can tell . . .

Then came the fun part—filling the bar's lubrication boots with grease.

I had assumed that Seven assembly would be a grubby job, but most of the time it seemed almost the opposite. If a part hasn't seen a single road mile, if you install it straight out of the box, how can it get dirty? I *felt* dirty pretty fast, though, and more like a mechanic once I stuck my hands in the

Quaker State grease tub. It looked disgusting—like something you'd found, and wished you hadn't, in a barnyard—but felt like thick skin cream and smelled only slightly rancid. Totting up the many tasks to be performed—screwing in bolts, tightening nuts, easing holes, installing studs—and the slippery liquids to apply—grease, oil, rubber lubricant, silicone spray, antiseize, Loctite—car mechanics was beginning to manifest a significant sexual undertone.

The downside of grease soon made itself apparent. The boots were secured with four synthetic-rubber O-rings, and they were difficult to handle with slippery fingers. Moreover, they proved almost impossible to stretch into place, a thirty-degree day turning them rigid and unyielding . . . and bringing to mind the frozen O-rings that doomed the space shuttle *Challenger.* Chris, when I broke down and called, suggested I place the rings in hot water to make them more flexible. The immersion did the trick—though I suppose I'll always retain, on the edge of consciousness, a mental picture of the Seven blowing up because of a tiny, overstressed rubber circle. That's impossible, of course, in real life . . . but after you've built a car yourself, hey, nothing seems impossible.

In putting the Seven together I had seen myself, however dimly, following a path trailblazed by Thoreau and given new life, more than a century later, by Robert Pirsig in *Zen and the Art of Motorcycle Maintenance.* The need to go back to basics; to learn by doing; to recognize that the head and the hand know very different things, and in very different ways. It was congenial territory, because a couple years earlier I had published a book on legal education exploring—I appreciated in retrospect—a parallel theme.

A year in law school had taught me the limitations of logical analysis. To stress—overstress—one way of understanding life was dangerous, sharpening the mind only by narrowing it;

to teach that law's core value was *reason*—a product almost exclusively of the head—rather than *justice*—created by both head and heart—was a social disservice. Logic should play a role in culture, it goes without saying, but at some point reason must give way to reality. If our legal system were truly interested in justice, for example, wouldn't lawyers be apportioned by lot rather than ability to pay? Does anyone doubt that clients shelling out $600 an hour are more likely to prevail in legal disputes than those who can afford only $60? $20? Zero?

Building the Seven, I realized, was backlash from my law-school experience, a way to satisfy a visceral need for deeper feeling, broader thinking. A hunger to follow natural laws that brooked no dissent.

Thoreau was an obvious touchstone. And Pirsig, too, for his mechanical bent. But Simone Weil? She hadn't even been on my radar screen, appearing only when I stumbled across a reference to her auto-factory work. But the more I looked into her writing, the larger Weil loomed, because she—much more than Thoreau or Pirsig—had a social conscience.

Weil wasn't following her own best grain when she donned overalls for Renault, as Thoreau did when he built his cabin or Pirsig when he fixed his motorbike. She was going against personal inclination, her goal not to put ideas into action—to "reduce a fact of the imagination to be a fact to his understanding," as Thoreau put it—but to determine whether her beliefs had real, honest weight. *Walden* and *Zen and the Art. . .* lose some luster once you've encountered Weil, because those books reveal themselves to be, in part, parables of will; the need to prove, dominate, control, even avenge. Weil went into the wide, wide world—to the Renault factory, later into battle during the Spanish Civil War—to dash her own preconceptions and predilections, not to realize them.

Weil set herself a difficult task. She was shy, clumsy,

socially awkward, and involuntarily eccentric; a sympathetic teacher referred to her as "the Martian," while a friend described Weil as "a strange mixture of coldness and passion," both "more human than anyone else" and "forbid[ding] herself all weakness." As an adult she was a communist, dedicated to improving the common lot, and maintained that desire even as she gave up communism for Catholicism. That's one reason she developed an antipathy to political parties, and to the established church as well—because every organization seemed to end up serving, sooner or later, its own interests.

Weil's writing is difficult, sometimes virtually unreadable. But that's a function of her relentless devil-wrestling . . . and she took on perhaps the most baffling demon of them all, the riddle of identity. Weil never established where the culture ended and the individual began—who could?—but recognized the centrality of the question. And that a culture should be the sum of its individual members, not an abstract set of ideas, values, prejudices, before which individuals bowed. Gee: Perhaps Patrick McGoohan, between takes on the set, was sitting in the director's chair flipping through . . .

The more I read about Weil, the more I identified with her. (Identification? She'd cringe at the thought.) Intellectually and politically, at first; then personally and psychologically. For Weil, like me, came from a cultured, liberal, well-off family, one that revered books and lively conversation, in which academic success was presumed. I couldn't help feeling, after a time, that I was lying on John's garage floor for the same reasons Weil worked at the Renault factory: because I wasn't compelled to. We left the library out of guilt, in part, but mostly from a nagging belief that answers can't be found in books alone, that thought and action are interdependent, must be allowed to modify one another. To restrict oneself to thinking, or to acting, was to renounce half the world.

Attempting to track down Weil's frame of mind, and thus

perhaps my own, I began to read one of her last writings, *The Need for Roots*. Much of it is fascinating, beginning with the title. For one thing, Weil blamed France's malaise following World War II on the excesses of the French Revolution, arguing that its emphasis on individual rights led directly to the cults of personality, and concentrations of power, of this century. It was a strange, unexpected analysis, and prompted many new questions—mostly about the notion of relevance. Wasn't I building a car? Examining the history of the automobile? *What the hell was I doing in eighteenth-century Paris?*

The most famous epigraph in modern English literature is probably "Only connect," used by E. M. Forster in the novel *Howard's End*. The book illuminates the gulf between art and commerce, city and country, progress and tradition, act and thought (a character is killed by a falling bookcase). It is also a plea to look with universal eyes. The world is a web; pluck a thread and the vibrations are felt not just here, and there, but everywhere. And so it is with books, and car building, anything at all; look hard enough, long enough, and the connections show themselves.

I had good cause to be in Jacobin France.

Henry Ford's development of the moving assembly line didn't occur in a vacuum. It was predicated on many other things, including plenty of workers, material resources, and consumer capital. Above all, however, it was grounded on the notion of standardized parts. "The way to make automobiles," Ford said in 1903, "is to make one automobile like another automobile . . . just like one pin is like another pin when it comes from a pin factory."

Ford probably didn't realize he was paying homage, in the passage above, to Adam Smith. The Scot illustrated his celebrated theory of the division of labor, after all, with a description of high-output pin manufacturing—an example Smith liked so much he used it twice, in both *The Wealth of Nations* and its less famous predecessor, the *Lectures on Jurisprudence*. Ford read neither book, one can assume, but he certainly understood Smith's economic ideas. Standardized parts—which hinted at hyperdivided labor, assembly lines, and interchangeability—were key to Ford's mass-production goal.

And who invented standardized, interchangeable parts? Back to revolutionary France; the credit is usually given to a Parisian metalworker named Honoré Le Blanc. In 1785 the U.S. ambassador to France learned of Le Blanc's interchangeable-part musket, visited his workshop, and became so enthusiastic about the weapon that he urged Le Blanc to emigrate to America. The metalworker refused . . . but the ambassador was determined that a similar musket would be produced, some day, in his native land. And that day was not long in coming, for fifteen years later the ambassador, Thomas Jefferson, was president of the United States.

Jefferson picked Eli Whitney for the job. Whitney was already famous for inventing the cotton gin but nearly broke, nonetheless, from pursuing Southern patent pirates. He hasn't done well historically, either; in recent decades Whitney's been called "a song-and-dance man," even a charlatan, for obtaining government contracts to deliver interchangeable-part muskets well before designing the necessary technology.

Weil, an eccentric and an exile, longed for roots, as the treatise mentioned above makes clear. But can someone be too rooted? Eli Whitney was a friend and student of Yale divinity professor Elizur Goodrich, my great-great-great-great-great grandfather; he married the granddaughter of Jonathan Edwards, the Puritan theologian after whom my residential college at Yale was named; Elizur Goodrich Jr., Yale's first law professor, attended the 1801 meeting at which Whitney showed President-elect Jefferson his plans for a standardized-part musket. Whitney even spent the night in

Brookfield, Connecticut, where I now live, on his way to New Haven—in 1789, of all years—to enroll at Yale. I wish I could say, to complete the circle, I often drive by Whitney's stopping place, but that's not the case . . . though I may have paddled over it, since the section of town he stayed in lies underwater, wiped out by a 1950s dam.

My ancestors almost certainly invested in what would become the Whitney firearms plant at Mill Rock, just outside New Haven. (At the very least, Elizur Goodrich Jr. signed a security bond on Whitney's behalf "to encourage the manufacture" of his friend's musket.) It's bad enough, as a lifelong leftist, to learn that family members played a significant role in the mass-production of guns; it's worse to learn they helped inaugurate a chain of events leading to the deskilling, the commodification, of labor. Worst of all, though, is discovering that Whitney was fully conscious, even then, of eliminating craftsmen from the manufacturing process.

One goal of his musket making, he wrote, was "to substitute correct and effective operations of machinery for that skill of the artist which is acquired only by long experience." More: He hoped to trap workers in his mass-production mold by hiring family men with "perhaps some little property to fix them in place, who consequently cannot be easily removed to any considerable distance." Let's put things in their darkest light. I'm building an automobile by hand today because my forebears, nearly two centuries ago, aspired to eliminate such work. Like Ford with Greenfield Village, perhaps I'm building the Seven as a form of penance.

6

HOLLOWING OUT
THE CORE

Fordism and Taylorism are often confused. Both stressed efficiency, eradicated job satisfaction, and fostered unskilled labor. The two systems also subdivided work into small, meaningless tasks, to a degree that sometimes defies belief. Frank Gilbreth coined the term *therblig* (an almost-backwards anagram of his name) to describe indivisible units of thought or motion, and used them to show footwear clerks, for example, how to "take a customer's shoe off in seven seconds, and put it back on again and lace it up in twenty-two seconds." (At home, he demonstrated that bringing a razor to one's shaving-creamed face entailed six distinct therbligs.) Ford, for his part, divided the assembly of a fly-wheel magneto into twenty-nine distinct operations, of a motor into eighty-four. The result was an enormous increase in production—and a similar decrease in Ford-employee morale, as workers began to see themselves as tiny cogs in a giant machine.

But there's a significant difference between Fordism and Taylorism, and it explains why the former dominates industrial culture. While Taylor concentrated almost exclusively on production, Ford knew the equation contained another element: Why make more products more efficiently if few people had the cash to buy them? So Ford worked both sides of the problem, dedicating himself to creating consumers as well as consumables. If Ford's production revolution commenced in 1913 with the installation of the first moving assembly line, his consumer revolution—which has proved of even greater significance—began the following year, when Ford introduced the Five-Dollar Day. In one fell swoop, in the middle of a depression, he doubled the average industrial salary in the United States.

Although the general public was thrilled by the Five-Dollar day, American business was shocked to its core. *The Wall Street Journal* called Ford "immoral"; an employers' association in Detroit accused Ford of undermining capitalism; a prominent heiress said Ford's policy would foment worker ambition and thus revolution; individual businessmen condemned Ford as a "mad socialist" and "a traitor to his class." Even Ford's own executives, arm-twisted into agreement, thought the across-the-board raise would destroy the company. It defied then-standard economic theory—that subsistence wages, having been ratified by the labor marketplace, were optimal. Why pay more for a worker than you have to, or charge less for a product than the market will bear?

Ford's contemporaries failed to see that the Five-Dollar Day—which also reduced daily working hours from ten to eight—was born of practicality, not compassion. In 1913, the year the Highland Park assembly line began operating, Ford had to hire 53,000 workers to keep his workforce steady at 14,000; by 1915, Ford had to hire only 6,508—most of them expansion workers, not replacements. The precipitous drop in turnover resulted partly from a reform prohibiting foremen from firing workers at will, but it was mostly due to the new high wages. Ford jobs, like most in the auto industry today, had become so well paid that workers found them very difficult to quit.

It wasn't clear at the time, but the Five-Dollar Day was, for workers, a Trojan horse. It demonstrated conclusively that they could be bought off—that labor could be stripped, with little protest, of everything but monetary value. The Five-Dollar Day made the paycheck the definitive test of a job's worth, blasting forever the notion that work could be its own reward.

Henry Ford is regarded with contempt in many quarters today. Sometimes for good reason: His anti-Semitism, for example, was deep, lasting, public, and proselytizing, not to mention ignorant. Ford was the first to publish in English, through a newspaper he owned, the fraudulent *Protocols of the Elders of Zion*, and helped legitimize the mindless bigotry that brought forth Nazism. Few historians believe Ford supported Hitler financially in the 1920s, but he certainly provided "moral" aid and comfort, was praised as a paragon in *Mein Kampf*, and accepted from Hitler, in 1938, the Supreme Order of the German Eagle. During World War II Ford recanted his anti-Semitism . . . but not for the first time, and for no better reason, quite possibly, than its being bad for business.

Ford's anti-Semitism, like most prejudices, is hard to explain. But it may well have arisen from his associating Jews with bankers and money, two things Ford heartily disliked.

It's strange to think that the world's first billionaire disdained money, but that seems to be the case; Ford regarded money, quite sincerely, as a necessary evil. "The money influence—the pressing to make a profit on an 'investment,'" he wrote in his autobiography, ". . . seemed to be at the bottom of most troubles"; it led not to better products but "neglect of or skimping of work and hence of service." In trying to operate his first two automobile companies Ford saw money as more obstacle than incentive. "Everything had to be planned to make money," he wrote: "the last consideration was the work."

It's important to distinguish Ford's anti-Semitism from his antibanker and antimoney attitudes because the latter prejudices proved prescient. Ford financed his company out of operating profits for more than a decade, an almost unheard-of feat ensuring that engineers, not financiers, ran the firm. One result of that independence was improved quality across the automotive board; his contemporaries were forced—as their descendants would be, half a century later, by Japanese competition—to improve their vehicles. Ford also refused to sell cars on the installment plan until 1928, a decade after General Motors started the practice, because he feared time sales would break the link between production and consumption. History confirmed the apprehension: Consumer credit increased dramatically in the 1920s, most of it going into automobile loans, and many new car owners—having experienced the wonders of financing—decided to purchase stock on credit, too. If the rest of the car industry had shared Ford's aversion to debt, in other words, we might have avoided the market crash of 1929, the Great Depression, and—just possibly—World War II.

Ford knew instinctively that money "hollowed out the core of things," as philosopher Georg Simmel once wrote. That it quantified the unquantifiable; flattened the three dimensions of life to the single dimension of economics, ensured—among other things—that entities incapable of commercial valuation would be deemed worthless. Money might be a universal language, but it was a lowest-common-denominator tongue, a grammar that reduced important things to figures in a ledger book. (Ford didn't like ledgers, either: It's no myth, apparently, that even into the 1940s the company's operating costs were estimated, sometimes, by weighing invoices on a scale.) Yet Ford instituted the Five-Dollar Day regardless, hoping to retain the advantages of well-paid labor by making good wages contingent on behavior deemed—by Ford, of course—acceptable.

Ford's Sociological Department encouraged workers to avoid alcohol and gambling, to save earnings for future home purchases, to shop economically, to shun installment purchases. And the workers went along . . . for a time.

In 1921, seven years after its inception, the Sociological Department (by then renamed the Educational Department) was shut down, "the money influence" having caught up with Ford once more. The company's profits had declined dramatically during World War I; Ford's executives insisted on cutbacks and the elimination of unprofitable ventures; workers had begun to resent being patronized, to note inflation's erosive effect on wages (which seemed ordinary, anyway, by then). Ford's semifeudal state was dying, its semibenevolent despot unable to control the forces—the discretionary money, the consumerism—he had unleashed. His dream was gradually turning sour; Ford's fantasies of cleanliness (the maintenance staff at the River Rouge plant once numbered five thousand) and service (Ford's schools, supermarkets, hospital, and credit union were groundbreaking organizations) could no longer excuse a deeper manipulation.

The same kind of manipulation, be it noted, that Number Six encountered in The Village.

The best satire on Fordism is found in Aldous Huxley's *Brave New World*, published five years after the Model T was discontinued, in 1932. In that book the Christian god has been replaced by Henry Ford, crucifixes having been trimmed to create "the sign of the T," and modern years are designated "A.F.," After Ford. An important administrator is called "his fordship," hours are tolled by the giant clock Big Henry, Eton boasts a metal statue of Our Ford, and people talk in revised clichés: "Ford's in his flivver, all's well with the world." The culture is purely utilitarian, for its leaders have decided that anomie is preferable to autonomy. Citizens are genetically engineered, mass-produced like any other product: Conceived in vials, reared in huge nurseries, and hypnotically conditioned throughout their youth, they are programmed to accept unthinkingly the strict class roles—and work—to which they are assigned. Most citizens consider themselves happy but in fact are brainwashed, adult children living out their lives in "an invisible bottle of infantile and embryonic fixations."

Aldous Huxley had seen, sooner than most, the consequences of Ford's vision. Since the flip side of mass production is mass consumption, consumer habits were the next variable inviting the capitalist's attention; and mind, as a bonus, was more readily controlled than matter (Hitler was already demonstrating as much). So the people of *Brave New World* do little but labor, consume, "vacation" with the drug *soma*, and play equipment-heavy sports. ("Imagine," says one character, "the folly of allowing people to play elaborate games which do nothing to increase consumption.") Work, what's more, is itself degraded, merely make-work, because all labor-saving devices have been mothballed; work exists only to limit leisure, because free time leads to independent thought and thus to social unrest. Huxley's modern man is a self-made pawn, a creature of the system taught from birth—

"decanting," here—that "everyone belongs to everyone else."

Ford's Sociological/Educational Department was not, of course, as bad as all that. But its demise didn't indicate growing management sensitivity; it marked, instead, a hardening of industrial practices. As the last director of the Educational Department wrote—in a biography of Henry Ford, no less—his job had become irrelevant to a company increasingly convinced "that men are more profitable to an industry when driven rather than led, that fear is a greater incentive to work than loyalty."

I was in college, acquiring all sorts of impractical information I would never come close to using, when I began to appreciate my automotive illiteracy. Driving back to the dorm after a soccer game one afternoon I heard a terrible racket, *bang-bang-bang-bang-bang*, issuing from the Datsun's rear end. I should have stopped immediately, but didn't, suffering from the auto idiot's classic panic response: If I ignore the problem, maybe it will go away.

I reached the dorm, slowly and noisily, and soon ascertained the cause of my difficulty. The right-rear wheel was bouncing back and forth on its studs, the mechanic who rotated the tires that morning having failed to tighten the lug nuts. I could have killed the mechanic—or rather he could have killed me, for the nuts eventually would have unscrewed completely, or the studs sheared off. The classic cartoon scene: a driver—Goofy, no doubt—watching a runaway tire pass him on the freeway, then suddenly realizing (bug-eyed double take) it's his own.

On that day I resolved to fix my car, whenever possible, myself. The thought came almost on the level of philosophy: *Why should I pay someone else to fuck up my car when I can fuck it up* personally *for free?*

The decision had a soft center, however. Soon I was too

busy with graduate school, and then employment, to be happy spending my few spare hours in a garage. Occasionally I performed routine maintenance: changing the oil or cleaning spark plugs, replacing a water pump or setting engine timing. At the time the work felt like blows against the empire, but in retrospect it seems an attempt to confront my fears of, and exasperation with, specialized knowledge.

Yes, the land of the free and the home of the brave . . . yet every day I was bombarded, subtly or aggressively and everything in between, by voices telling me how to think about the world. About the news, by journalists and journalism professors; about justice, by lawyers and politicians; about some mechanical or electrical device, by some mechanic or electrician. Did a week go by in which I wasn't expected to jettison some preference, some intuition, some judgment, in deference to another's supposedly authoritative opinion?

I lacked the ability, obviously, to trust. In theory that wasn't a flaw; it's important for reporters to take nothing on faith. But I seemed to have overdone the doubt, shaded into constant suspiciousness, perhaps because I felt no solid ground beneath my feet. That became apparent rather quickly in journalism school, where within weeks I was looking at journalism with the same skepticism journalists generally reserve for their subjects. At least one professor was shocked, *shocked* by my do-you-really-think-so? questions, as if I were betraying the brotherhood.

I had chosen a career, and wanted to love it, but couldn't help noting on a daily basis that the top television news stories, the newspaper headlines, the narrative structure of news reports, often weren't about "the news" at all. They were, just as frequently, about the reporters' access, their "exclusives"; about spinning facts, pleasing demographic segments. The news was always tailored in some fashion—by a reporter's ambitions to make the front page, the news station's desire to broaden its audience, the writer's need to hook the reader or viewer. And such tailoring was actively encouraged by the profession, taught not as a necessary compromise but as an important skill.

My frustration with specialized, members-only information wouldn't take center stage until I entered law school (on a one-year fellowship for journalists). There my skepticism flowered, for it was clear almost immediately that neither the theory of law, nor its teaching methods, jibed with legal practice; clear to me at least, since I didn't intend to become an attorney and had no need to conceal my doubts. By the end of the year, having lived through two semesters of legal education and reconsidered four semesters of journalism school, I had begun to see that specialized education teaches students to use proprietary knowledge to acquire power; to favor professional goals over the public interest. And I likewise grasped this equation's analogue—that information controlled by one person or group creates ignorance in others . . . an ignorance that's eminently exploitable.

It's frightening, the idea that information creates ignorance. But there's a saving grace, too; the fact that ignorance, once admitted, can be remedied. Surely that's one root of my restlessness—that I'm always finding something I'd rather not be ignorant about.

7

WAYS OF KNOWING

The doctor wasn't kidding. Upon completing the front suspension I discovered in the bottom of the relevant hardware bag two heavy, brass-colored nuts. They bore odd, slashing notches on either side that oozed importance; did the grooves act, perhaps, as built-in lockwashers, or route the nut-binding safety wire used by racers? Or were the furrows a nod to weight saving, like perforated gas pedals? Or simply decorative? I hadn't a clue.

The nuts, fortunately, were identical to those I had used to secure the front steering arms. There seemed only two possibilities: that the nuts were duplicates, or might be needed somewhere in the rear suspension. The second possibility seemed unlikely, though, for the rear end didn't have steering arms, since the Seven was not a four-wheel-steered vehicle (such beasts do exist). Might the extra nuts be a trick, a test, a diversion, someone's idea of a joke (*if he's done the inventory, he'll know what to make of 'em*)? On the other hand, maybe it was just the New Math (these days, I suppose, the Passé Math): A Seven less Two nuts is a One-car accident waiting to happen.

I blithely declared the nuts redundant, reasoning (again blithely) that the rear suspension was too different from the front's to require identical parts. That's the case in most cars, since for decades the axles divided the workload in predictable fashion; the front set of wheels took care of the steering, and the rear set, propulsion. In recent years that's all changed, what with front-wheel drive and four-wheel drive and all-wheel drive—but the Seven, naturally, remains rear-wheel-driven . . . and thus happily stuck in the past.

You could almost say the Seven's going backward in time. Many come equipped with a De Dion tube, an exotic-sounding rear suspension device that the average Joe might expect to encounter in reference to, say, Formula 1 racers. In reality the De Dion tube, like the Seven itself, is an anachronism, having been invented in the 1890s by one Monsieur Trepardoux, brother-in-law to the Bouton of the pioneering car company De Dion–Bouton. Until that time most cars had borrowed the primitive rear suspensions of horse-drawn carts, which couldn't easily accommodate the added weight of a drive train—especially the very hefty differential, which redirects the driveshaft's spin to the wheels.

But De Dion–Bouton had a special problem: Its steam-powered cars were also steam braked, so in back they were especially heavy. Trepardoux solved the weight issue by bolting the differential to the chassis itself and adding to the suspension a hollow tube that acted like a "dead" rear axle. It may seem unfair that he didn't get his name on this ingenious solution, but in the long run his employer, the count, proved deserving. Trepardoux, angry that the boss had decided to abandon steam in favor of gasoline engines, quit De Dion–Bouton in 1894—and probably regretted the decision soon after. By the turn of the century De Dion–Bouton was producing the world's best-selling car, a gas-powered tricycle, and by 1902 had sold some twenty-six thousand vehicles.

In the De Dion system the differential is no longer unsprung weight (that's a good thing, I'm told). Driveshafts still run to the wheels from each side of the differential, but the De Dion tube now positions the wheels in relation to the road. The net effect is a better-handling car, although—in stark contrast to the Seven's front suspension—it's attained without élan. In theory the De Dion system is a clever compromise between fully independent rear suspension and live-axle suspension ("live" characterizing an axle that transmits power), but in practice the balance is difficult to obtain. As one of my British car books puts it, in what I assume is British-engineer-deadpan prose, "The [De Dion] ideal is rarely achieved, geometrical solecisms being as common in the location of a dead beam axle as in that of the live variety."

The Seven manual offered two ways of dealing with the De Dion tube: attaching its accessory parts first, outside the car, or bolting it, bare, directly onto the chassis. Either way, the tube couldn't go in until the differential had been installed, a fairly straightforward operation. Except, of course, for the hacksaw.

When you think about automotive tools, you usually think of specialized instruments—timing lights, compression gauges, tach-dwell meters. It was disconcerting, consequently, to find that the first tool I'd be using, wrenches aside, was something last employed on a rusty nail. A metal file, sure, or extrafine steel wool . . . but a hacksaw? A tad crude for Seven work, I thought, but there was no choice: Unless the differential lost nearly an inch from its backside mounting lug, the differential would puncture the De Dion tube (which moves up and down with the wheels) the first time I drove over a large bump.

This minor surgery carried major significance. Lop off too much lug and you've put a hole in the differential housing; too little and there's soon a hole in the De Dion tube. More to the point, though, the operation forced me to approach a problem in an unfamiliar way. I usually work on impulse—a tendency born of the need to bypass my brain, which produces an astonishing variety of second thoughts. But impulsiveness wouldn't do at this moment, for building a car is a one-shot deal. All those second thoughts, here, could literally save my life, which meant I had to deal with them up front.

I lifted the differential—conceived, incidentally, by Leonardo da Vinci, though not embodied until 1828 by a Frenchman—from its shipping box, re-re-re-reread the trimming instructions, and hoisted it onto the transmission crate. I labored deliberately, by measuring twice and sawing once (as carpenters say), and then by paying attention to the cut itself. The tortoise approach proved extremely satisfying: Having marked the amputation precisely, I didn't need to finesse the saw stroke and so could concentrate on the movement of the tool, the angle of the blade.

For a time I lived entirely in the moment, committing the straightest, smoothest sawing I've ever done. I fell easily into a rhythm, cutting deeply on the pull stroke and shallowly on the push, listening to the steady growl of a good pass, watching the ghostly clouds of aluminum dust float off into the air. In three or four minutes I was done and got nervous—were these tertiary thoughts? second thoughts once removed?— only toward the end, when the saw blade began to resonate with strange, watery tones. I was just learning how to play a tune when the lug-end came free, reddened from saw-blade paint.

There's much to be said for improvisation, but also for plans executed just so.

Like many other parts in the Seven, the diff—as car people refer to the differential—is made by Ford. That's another of the Seven's endearing qualities—its being an amalgam of components produced by other manufacturers, adapted or uprated (automobile-ese for "improved") or otherwise modified to suit. Another nice but little-known quality is Caterham's ability to undersell the original maker, meaning you may be able to buy a Ford gearbox more cheaply from Caterham than from your local Ford dealer.

Colin Chapman wouldn't take offense if you characterized the Seven as "cobbled together." That's exactly how Chapman began his auto-manufacturing career—buying old, decrepit cars and rebuilding them in a relative's garage outside London. The first Lotus, the Mark I, was a modified 1930 Austin Seven (note the name), a tiny, cheap, very popular, latter-day Model T whose stock version had among the lowest top speeds of any modern automobile. (The first BMW car was an Austin Seven built under license.) Chapman transformed his first Austin into a "special," or weekend racing car, in 1948, and was soon rebuilding others for fellow racers. Sometimes he added new components—alloy-bonded plywood to the Austin's frame, for example, to make it stronger and more rigid—but usually modified parts salvaged from unrelated cars.

Chapman's ingenuity was on a par with Ford's, at the very least, and more interesting, mechanically speaking, because directed at the car itself rather than car production. He cured the Austin Seven's habitual oversteer by installing its rear axle *upside down;* he changed an axle ratio by putting incompatible gears in a transmission and substituting *metal polish* for oil. Given the success of these experiments, it's no surprise to learn that Chapman often said, "The trouble with experts is they know what can't be done." It's no surprise, either, that the idea echoes Ford, who wrote that the company had to "get rid of a man as soon as he thinks himself an expert—because no one ever considers himself an expert if he really knows his job."

Necessity would eventually become the mother of invention at the Lotus works, but initially, because Chapman had no capital, it generated simple parsimony. Chapman had other reasons for frugality, however, even after Lotus flourished; he had a jet-set lifestyle to subsidize and a money-burning race team. (He wasn't above malfeasance, either, as became evident after his death: An investor in the DeLorean sports car, Chapman apparently converted a few million pounds of company funds to personal use.) Chapman was so cheap, in fact, he was said to sleep with lists of van and light-truck parts under his pillow, since industrial components usually cost less than their passenger-car equivalents.

Caterham continues the all-the-parts-that-fit tradition, despite the company's being forced, as the years go by and components age and disappear, to do more and more designing on its own. Remove the aluminum and fiberglass from my Seven, though, and a Ford mechanic would feel right at home.

The engine's valve covers may read "1700 SuperSprint," for example, but they're mounted on the same "Kent" block, modified with larger cylinders, used in Ford's U.S. Pintos and English Cortinas. The block proved extraordinarily rugged—it was produced into the 1990s and is still used in logging camps as a generator—but Chapman chose the engine in part for its easy availability; the one he settled on for the Seven's immediate predecessor, the prototype Mark VI, was so hard to come by at first that Lotus built motors from parts scavenged at Ford dealers. In the Seven the Kent block replaced the Coventry Climax, a famous racing engine originally

designed as a fire pump . . . but best known for having a likeness of Lady Godiva molded into its valve covers. That's why
Lotus drivers go so fast, the joke goes—because they're chas-
ing the naked lady.

Narrow your eyes when stepping into Caterham's shop in
Dartford, Kent, and you might be back in 1950, or even 1910.
No assembly line, no giant pneumatic rivet guns, just a dozen
or so jig-raised chassis in various stages of production; the air
is clean, the noise minimal, the workers' pace unhurried. An
automobile *factory*? No, you can't call it that; the place is a
workshop, populated by craftsmen rather than technical specialists, sports-car lovers rather than wage slaves.

Simon Eade, Caterham's customer-relations agent, gave
me a tour of the works. The shop is small, could be hidden in
an ordinary industrial park—which it is, off the M24 motor-
way two hours from central London. The only thing setting
Caterham apart from the other facilities in the neighborhood
is the inordinate number of neat-looking roadsters parked out
front, many owned by employees. Sitting next to the Sevens,
the VW Passat I'd driven here looked like a tank.

Caterham was about to introduce its latest Seven, the
Vauxhall-powered version. The engine, the first from-the-
ground-up European power plant in many years, had its
cylinder head tweaked for Caterham by the racing specialists
at Cosworth Engineering—an appropriate touch, for Cosworth was founded in 1958 by two Lotus employees, Mike
Costin and Kevin Duckworth. (The late Frank Costin, Mike's
brother, was also a Lotus alum, and the "cos" of the English
specialty-carmaker Marcos.)

"Nice, isn't it?"

Simon was pointing to a raised display of the Vauxhall
motor, which was about as handsome as automobile engines
get.

"The Rover engine that's coming," Simon continued, "it's all aluminum, not just the cam covers. You could almost pick it up by yourself."

The most noteworthy aspect of these engines, though, is their being catalytic-converter-ready. The Seven isn't sold as an already-built car in many countries because the standard engines can't pass, out of the box, modern emission-control standards. With a converter-bearing engine the Seven's market could increase exponentially . . . and growth, these days, appeals to Caterham, unable to resist the lure of market globalization. (Tradition, as Rolls-Royce recently found, takes you only so far.) The company has also introduced its first non-Seven model, a sleek, polished-aluminum, well-received roadster called the Caterham 21. The 21 even comes with—drumroll, *please*—doors.

Half of Caterham's Sevens go overseas, a huge proportion to Asia. Japanese car buffs have long been obsessed with the Seven—Japanese auto magazines seem to publish more articles on the Seven than their British counterparts—and bring in hundreds of factory-built models, usually Caterhams, every year.

"They like the 'ally,'" said Simon, walking me past a stack of unpainted aluminum bonnets. "They like the history, and they love the Seven because it's hand-built. They do everything on computers, the Japanese: They can't do it themselves."

Can't do it themselves—could that possibly be true, given the strong craft tradition in Japan? I had no idea, but it was indisputable that latter-day Japanese car manufacturing, while founded on the Fordist mass-production model, was tempered by the craftsman's love of quality. *No wonder they liked Sevens. . . .*

In a small warehouse Simon showed me a dozen assembled Sevens awaiting shipment. In another was a stack of shrink-wrapped chassis, recently arrived from their fabricator, Arch Motors. Arch is one of Caterham's two hundred suppliers, a figure that helps explain why the Seven, despite surface appearances, is constantly evolving: Caterham is a tiny account for most component manufacturers, so few hesitate before discontinuing a part that leaves Caterham scrambling. Arch, with Caterham its main customer, is the biggest exception to the rule. The destiny of the two companies is intertwined, a throwback to the days when craftworkers were simultaneously independent and interdependent, and very conscious of the social, commercial web that connected them.

After walking me past a few wrecks—mangled British Sevens, not surprisingly, usually end up here—Simon passed me on to Jez Coates, Caterham's technical director.

We had already met. Or I felt we had, at least, for Jez is the star (Seven aside) of the assembly videotape, which Chris had sent upon receiving my no-I'm-not-kidding deposit. I tagged along while Jez gave two Floridians, who hoped to establish a Seven racing series in the States, a production tour.

Most of the conversation was way over my head.

Yeah, the suspension geometry's better . . . altered the camber and toe-in . . . new spring rates, Bilsteins standard . . . double–shear set-up. . . sump's got foam baffles . . . evaporative–loss system . . .

The one scrap of information I seized on, like the drowning man a rope, pertained to the oil cooler. I had long questioned its being installed directly in front of the Seven's radiator, since the oil cooler in my old Lancia was set to one side: Didn't the Caterham layout reduce the radiator's cooling ability? (So what if there wasn't anyplace else to put it?) I asked one of Jez's assistants and learned that the one-behind-the-other position did as I suspected, reducing cooling efficiency by maybe 10 percent. Given that the Seven tended to overheat in traffic—a fact gleaned, I admit, from *The Prisoner*—I decided to skip the option.

My main memory of the Caterham works was its openness. You could practically walk off the street to tour the plant, and not only find its technical director under a car but ask him questions about it. Try doing that with an automobile built in Detroit or Tokyo or Stuttgart—or any product, for that matter. The Seven is one thing, unlike law or sausages or news, you don't regret seeing made.

At the factory, at least.

8

TO MARKET, TO MARKET

Ford was right—history *is* bunk. About history's ignoring harrows, without question; but also because it's written by the victors, and because it reflects, unavoidably and necessarily, the historian's point of view. You don't get tenure, or make the best-seller list, by reconfirming what colleagues, or readers, already know; instead you play crack-the-whip with the past, apply a new filter, reinterpret accepted understandings from the bottom up, sideways, askew. *Make it new:* Ezra Pound's imperative applies to history as well, even if "new history" is a paradox lost.

History once made a hero of Alfred P. Sloan Jr., long-time chairman of General Motors. In some circles he retains that rank: As the father of the modern corporation, industry's first and prototypical Organization Man, he has proved far more influential in the business world than Henry Ford (whose management practices ran from nonexistent to baleful). Sloan would never have said anything as inflammatory as "history is bunk" . . . except he did, though the malignance of his remark wasn't recognized for more than a decade. "The primary object of the corporation," Sloan wrote in 1964 and in direct repudiation of Henry Ford, "was to make money, not just to make motorcars."

Ford tried mightily to put the car before the horse, but never, like Sloan, the cart.

Sloan, an MIT graduate, started on the right track. In his early years, as head of the Hyatt Roller Bearing Company, he learned the importance of quality manufacturing at the feet of Henry Leland, general manager of Cadillac (a direct corporate descendant of Ford's second failed automobile company). Leland, who sold Cadillac to General Motors in 1908, had absorbed the value of precision engineering while working for two bastions of Whitney-inspired standardization—the Springfield Armory and Colt Arms—and wasn't about to change upon entering the automobile industry. When Sloan sent Leland an order of not-quite-perfect axle bearings, the future GM chairman reported in one of his autobiographies, Leland refused to accept delivery. "Mr. Sloan," he said, "Cadillacs are made to run, not just to sell."

In 1917 Leland founded the Lincoln Motor Car Company, having been forced out of General Motors (which bought Hyatt Roller Bearing the next year); within fifteen years, with Sloan at the helm, GM had explicitly rejected Leland's credo.

The evolution of Sloan's approach is comprehensible, if not entirely excusable. The Model T was a wonderful car for its time, but Ford's refusal to update the vehicle, improve it, gave other manufacturers the opportunity to surpass Ford—in sales, if not in quality. Ford stressed durability; Chrysler would eventually stress technology. And General Motors? Sloan, ever the company man, listened to executives who favored ornamentation over mechanics, contemporaneity over timelessness. In 1923 GM instituted the annual model change; in 1927 Sloan hired Harley Earl, car customizer to Hollywood film stars, to run GM's new Styling Section. In 1940 Sloan would describe his change of heart in the frankest terms: "We want to make you dissatisfied with your current car so you will buy a new one."

F. W. Taylor concentrated on production; Ford on consumption as well: Sloan on consumption especially, and on merchandising above all. Ford, naturally, was appalled, protesting that the annual model change sought "only to provide something new, not something better"; that his company built cars to last as long as possible, not to become instantly obsolete. "It is strange," Ford wrote the year of GM's first annual alteration, "how just as soon as an article becomes successful, somebody starts to think that it would be more successful if only it were different."

But that's what Sloanism did, and its consequences are felt every day. The auto industry spent $11.6 billion on advertising in 1996, according to a marketing annual; you can't pick up a magazine or newspaper without reading of a car that's better, newer, faster, more prestigious, more fashionable, more *something* than your own. Sloanism institutionalized the idea of selling the sizzle rather than the steak, and the result was a sea change in industrial culture. Workers had already been instructed how to produce, buyers how to consume; under Sloanism consumers would be trained to buy more and more of the things and services companies found most profitable to make.

Sloanism also affected workers, of course, and here the development was undeniably for the worse. The factory of the future, in Ford's imagination, was run by automated machines requiring few workers; specialized labor to beget the machines, and unskilled labor to watch over them. But Sloan's vision altered the Fordist factory's development, because the change-the-trim-every-year system created an enormous amount of unskilled make-work—well-paid make-work, to be sure, but make-work nonetheless. Computer-programmed machine tools would, in time, adjust the picture, but for decades Detroit led the world in the production of deadening, dead-end employment. While about 10 percent of industrial jobs in the United States were unskilled or semiskilled in the mid-1970s, automotive historian James Flink has written in his definitive history *The Automotive Age*, in carmaking the figure was 75 percent.

It's too bad Aldous Huxley didn't write a sequel to *Brave New World* that took on Sloanism. (*Brave New World Revisited*, published in 1958, is an outdated collection of not-very-compelling essays.) Sloanism, after all, represented a devaluation of work beyond that described in Huxley's 1932 novel. Pre-Ford, a worker could find at least some degree of individuality through labor; post-Sloan, work was presumed hollow. The worker, thereafter, was encouraged to find individuality in places like automobile showrooms—which provided, of course, not authentic individuality but its commercial surrogate.

Henry Ford believed people should live to work, as he did, but was the unwitting prime mover behind a world in which people worked, increasingly, just to live. Alfred Sloan, in turn, embraced this brave new world, realizing that a sharp distinction between work and leisure would benefit the corporation's bottom line.

Harley Shaiken, a professor of sociology who was once a GM machinist, bears witness. The contemporary skilled worker, he wrote in a book entitled *Disabling Professions*,

is demoted from a cog in the production process into a baby
sitter for a machine. Like any baby sitter, the machinist is
allowed to feed his subject, watch it, and clean up after it.

The effect, Shaiken writes, is that modern work becomes a
prison rather than a fulfillment, and time off "a parole whose
quality has already been determined by the sentence served. . . .
Leisure becomes a frenzied managed activity to forget the job
rather than a satisfying experience." And another opportunity,
need it be said, for marketers to sell more products.

Thoreau was ahead of his time in this area as well, criticizing modern work even in its early-industrial form. Why
spend "the best part of one's life earning money," he asked,
"in order to enjoy a questionable liberty during the least valu-
able part of it"? But that's what the typical worker does.

Like most people, First World through Third, I've held
jobs that depended on the delayed-gratification equation: dis-
agreeable work (now) + money (in two weeks) = enjoyment
(later). We did it because everyone else did, because we had
such hopes for the future, because we were indoctrinated with
the notion that money translates directly into pleasure. Frequently it did—but frequently it didn't, because working
inconsequentially five days a week, fifty weeks a year, seemed
to core one's vitality. Sometimes I could change gears after
leaving my cubicle at the state bar, all set to begin life anew,
but more often I carried the workday home, mostly in the
form of lamentation. *Surely my work could be more socially useful, more personally significant? If we dispensed with the hierarchy,
created a community, built a genuine sense of purpose . . .*

I lasted two years at *California Lawyer,* the longest I've
held a paycheck job. As a white-collar worker I was immune
to the worst forms of mind-numbing, soul-degrading, rou-
tinized labor, but I'd been Sloaned nonetheless . . . and didn't
like it one bit.

While assembling the Seven I worked a few hours a week at a publishing trade magazine, filling in for a friend on maternity leave. I liked the idea of balancing office work with garage work, exercising my mind one day and my spirit another ... but it didn't work out that way, for going to the magazine still meant slotting myself into a preexisting system. The optimal version of office work was lodged forever in my brain: a system that welcomed each new hire, teased out cooperatively the recruit's strengths, then used those strengths to improve the organization as a whole. The individual made adjustments, sacrifices, but so did the organizational chart.

The reality, of course, was fingers in dikes, hurry-up-and-waits, mysterious institutional goals, career gamesmanship, and conventional deference to the bottom line. I enjoyed an unusual degree of autonomy at the magazine, but my desk hours didn't seem to serve a broader, encompassing purpose.

Greet the receptionist, check the In box, visit with a colleague, sit at the cubicle; pick up the phone, gather some facts, log onto the computer, arrive at a facile conclusion; give or take or skip a meeting, monitor office politics, account for business pressures and others' deadlines. Wheels turned, big and small, and you moved with them—along for the ride, or speeding up one wheel, slowing down another, to keep the larger machine on track. And what kept the wheels moving was the wages and weekend dreams, not the rewards of intrinsically interesting work. Even as a reporter and critic, a shaper of perception for thousands, sometimes millions of readers, I felt the weight of weightlessness; of playing a game by rules over which I had no say.

Building the Seven couldn't have been more different. Its rules were those of nature, mostly, and they had substance; physical exactness counted here, on-the-fly accommodation was disdained. The Seven never left me at the mercy of competing agendas, didn't change when my back was turned; the car was always as I left it, aside from a few wind-blown leaves, a dead fly or five, and a million motes of dust. No one grew angry if I stopped working for a while; no one would know, or care, or suffer. I was totally responsible for my actions, answered only to myself—and, of course, the laws of physics.

It was a new kind of experience, working in John's garage, and strangely, a little like falling in love. Every act and thought seemed dramatic and significant, as if viewed through a magnifying glass. It was deeply satisfying to watch components come together, even if the coupling was shadowed by the knowledge that I wouldn't know for months, and perhaps never, whether the job was done correctly. I was like a child learning to write the alphabet: committing only chicken scratches, yet thrilled at the unfolding adventure, to be approaching untold secrets.

Some of those secrets, though, returned me to the very place from which I started. Which made me wonder, self-suspicious: Had I chosen this path for its circularity? Followed only familiar road signs, to ensure that I remained on native ground? Screened experience to deliver recognizable landmarks? I found connections, to be sure, in the unlikeliest places.

A major reason for building the Seven was to experience "flow"—to become so caught up in something that one's identity, rather than aggrandizing itself, seems to disappear. I primed the pump by reading the original book on the subject, psychologist Mihaly Csikszentmihalyi's *Flow: The Psychology of Optimal Experience*. During flow states, he writes, people attain a sense of mastery, "of participation in determining the content of life" that's otherwise absent. Flow states are commonly found in sports—when a baseball pitcher throws a perfect game, for example—but rarely on the job, because most work is too diffuse, too limited, or too managed to capture one's full attention.

From time to time I did get into the flow of things while building the Seven. But what I found fascinating about flow was less its existence than its meaning—that flow implied, at some level, rejection of a society's dominant values. A developed culture depends upon order and specialization, writes Csikszentmihalyi, with the result that citizens are routinely "forced to take on the habits and skills that the culture required, whether the individuals liked it or not." Searching for flow was a way of "reclaiming experience"; of repudiating the socialization that pushed people, hard, to "identify so thoroughly with the social order that they no longer can imagine themselves breaking any of its rules." Going with the flow, living in the moment, was an excellent way of "emancipating oneself from social controls."

Of course—*that* was the allure of the Seven, of *The Prisoner*, and of all my maverick friends, contemporary and historical. The expectations of the world "out there" rarely matched mine, so what remained was a distinct choice: to labor within the existing system and never find work satisfying, or without it in search of a unique, congenial flow.

9

GETTING MY BEARINGS

How, you ask, does the kit car assembler spend most of his time? Bolting? Installing? Adjusting? Thinking? Screwing his courage, perhaps, to the sticking place? None of the above: The correct answer is Waiting. And there are so many things to wait for—the replacement of missing parts, assembly-manual explications, new tools, more and different advice. And sometimes, merely inspiration. *If I wait long enough, maybe the light will dawn and I'll understand why I'm supposed to put that thing here, not there.* . . .

Chris Tchórznicki, thankfully, was always prepared to answer questions, reasonable and otherwise. While tightening some suspension bolts, for example, I discovered my 1/2-inch-drive torque wrench was incompatible with my

3/8-inch-drive sockets. The obvious solution was to purchase an adapter. But could I be sure, absolutely sure, the adapter wouldn't skew the torque readings?

Chris, like many car people, didn't sweat the small stuff, due to an instinctive feel for the correct mechanical move. "Not a problem," he said when I phoned about the adapter. "Should be the same. Just crank it to the proper reading and I'll have a look when you come up." I pictured bolts flying through the Seven's bonnet on some deserted back road in Massachusetts, but Chris knew best, right? He was one expert I could trust, mainly because he didn't act like one.

Thus reassured, I embarked upon a long and gratifying series of installations. Prop shaft to diff; diff to chassis; rear wheel half-shafts to diff and completed De Dion assembly; the wheels themselves. I was months from putting rubber on the road, but this still felt like progress.

Then came the rub. Minor trouble, at first: The differential's breather tube, which prevents differential fluid from becoming overpressurized, broke off when I tried to install it. Why? Maybe because I could never find the tube's "pips," which are supposed to align with . . . well, the manual never said. Which at least was consistent, since the pips—a word I associate with apples and Sherlock Holmes, and which my dictionary defines as "spot; speck"—seemed to be nonexistent, too.

Chris sent me another breather tube, and more importantly, an installation hint. Slip the breather tube through the hole in the back of a good-sized wrench socket; the socket provides purchase on the tube without stressing its sealing flange. A crafty maneuver, eminently logical, and just the sort of inside dope you're not likely to pick up on your own, that makes expertise expensive.

With the rear-wheel assemblies I hit a dead end. The roller bearings—the very part with which Alfred Sloan started making his automotive reputation—were to be installed in hub carriers, which in turn allow the half-shafts to spin without friction. It was easy to position the bearings by hand in the carriers, along with their races, but permanent installation required great pressure. The Seven manual says the bearings can be "gently tapped into place using a hammer and a suitable drift," but the only "drift" I knew was white, cold, and fluffy. Drift: it refers not just to snow, apparently, but anything of course! *driven*.

Who knew car assembly required frequent detours to the dictionary?

Chris to the rescue. He suggested I follow the example of Seven builders in England—"Run down to your local garage and see if they'll help out." In the background I could hear the clank of dropped tools, then Chris rummaging around at his shop desk: He must have answered my call while under a Seven. *What'd he do before portable phones?*

"Here we go, Akin. Ask for J. R." He gave me the number of Akin Racing in Ossining, New York, a few miles upriver from Hastings-on-Hudson. "I'll be running the Elite at Lime Rock next weekend, and Akin'll be there. I'll give J. R. the windscreen, and you can pick it up from him when you do the bearings."

Windscreen?

Chris had a laugh at that. I hadn't even noticed it was missing.

A few days later I was on my way to Akin in John's old VW. (The Rabbit is a story unto itself: The clutch slipped, the emergency brake and upshift lights had minds of their own, the gearshift knob read "1–2–3–4–E." *Extra*, perhaps?) Ossining is a larger version of Hastings, an old industrial town, but boasts one peculiarity I encountered quite by accident. I thought I had followed J. R.'s directions to the letter, but grew suspicious when I ended up on the wrong side of the tracks, literally; on a scenic road between the railway and the river.

I came to a huge, fenced-in compound, before which stood a rustic wooden sign reading . . . Sing Sing. *Ah, one of Henry Ford's training grounds!* Just think; some people paid vast sums for view property on the riverfront, and here it was free to anyone committing two, three felonies.

I found Akin Racing on my second pass through town. It was a candy store for the mechanically minded; sports cars and car parts, engines and chassis, machine tools and welding equipment, winches and tool chests—the sort of thing that make boys of any age drool. Not to mention the girlie calendars—quite modest at Akin, actually. In town an auto-supply store displayed a company magazine that featured a bikini-clad "Beauty of the Month."

J. R. Mitchell, well-known to Chris because he owned a Lotus Seven, was happy to help. "Last week, no way," he said, since Akin was getting ready for Lime Rock's season-opening race. The event took place despite snow flurries—no drifts, and Chris set a personal best.

As we walked to the hydraulic press I got a tour of the shop floor and saw all kinds of interesting cars, most of them vintage racers. A Lotus Eleven, one of the first streamlined, watermelon-seed-shaped cars and a reflection of Colin Chapman's aircraft background; a beautiful gray Fiat Seraglio; something called the "Silver Torpedo." There were other mystery vehicles as well, identifiable as race cars only because of the apselike roll bars protruding from their canvas covers.

I had brought the Seven assembly manual, and that was fortunate, since J. R. wanted to see an exploded diagram of the hub. J. R. had not encountered this particular design before: As the manual notes, my rear hubs were "specially modified" to enable the rear wheels to take the same brakes as the front. They were also covered with a protective coating, lending them a golden tint, which J. R. removed in a parts washer. Clean, the hubs shone with the soft gleam of burnished steel.

J. R. regreased the bearings and races, a job I had started in Hastings, and set each bearing in its hub carrier. He then put one of the embryonic assemblies into the hydraulic press—an upright "bottle" jack set in a frame with springs on either side—and positioned the outer hub on top, tapping it into place with a rubber mallet. Rummaging in a nearby box, he soon came up with the proper drifts: one, placed under the assembly, to make the pressing area flat, and the other, above, through which to apply force.

"You can get up to 15,000 psi," J. R. said, "but the whole thing vibrates like you wouldn't believe at about 10,000." Bearings didn't require compression anywhere near that high, he continued, greater pressures needed primarily for disassembling rusted, recalcitrant parts.

After the bearings were properly compressed—you pulled a lever on the press's side, much like the levers on Vegas's one-armed bandits—J. R. showed me his current project. On a workbench was the rear axle from a mid-1960s Series 2 Seven, which J. R. was adapting for installation on another Seven. "It's a real pain," he said, but clearly liked the challenge, not least because the modification forced him to focus his abilities, to rethink the suspension principles involved. "Yeah, like Colin Chapman," J. R. said. "You try this, try that, and eventually come up with something that works."

It's difficult to believe, in hindsight, that I bought a Seven before driving one. But I did, perhaps because the press reports were utterly convincing—good evidence of the selling power of magazine road tests.

And which played a major role, naturally, in Lotus's marketing strategy. Graham Arnold has written that he always tried to obtain "the maximum number of rave road tests" for Lotus through "several specially prepared press cars," and that's another tradition carried on by Caterham. In 1991, for example, Caterham loaned its top-of-the-line "HPC" Seven to a *Sports Car International* writer, who in turn provided the company with its best review ever; he compared the car's ride to BMW, its structural integrity to Porsche, engineering to Lamborghini, and build quality to Rolls-Royce (is there an inside joke here I don't get?). The designation HPC, not coincidentally, is canny promotion in and of itself; it's an acronym for the two-day High Performance Course that buyers must take to ensure they can handle the car.

I first drove a Seven during Lime Rock's annual Labor Day vintage-car races. It's an amazing event, and unlike most big-name auto racing, relentlessly amateur, in the good sense. Most participants trailer their rides—familiar marques like Triumph, Healey, and Alfa as well as nearly pure racers like Cunningham and Allard—but many compete in the same car in which they arrive. They do so because this kind of racing celebrates history as much as competition: Engineers and mechanics, drivers and devotees, are more important at Lime Rock's Vintage Festival than money and fame and international rankings. (There's an official "vintage" wine, too—made just down the street from my house, which sits on—don't wince—the Connecticut Wine Trail.) Many attendees stay in nearby hotels or B and Bs, but just as many camp out in tents, thrilled to be near the old, well-loved two-seaters of their childhood dreams. At least one regular has it both ways; he camps, yes—in a customized tour bus, complete with washing machine in the erstwhile luggage compartment.

Chris Tchórznicki often races a '54 Lotus VI at Lime Rock . . . though only when his wife allows it, for Mari is the car's primary driver. But race days are perfect for selling Sevens, too, so Chris always parks an immaculate demonstrator in the track's paddock, where it is soon surrounded by admirers (the majority over thirty-five or under twelve). Occasionally someone asks for a ride, and if the inquirer seems serious, and Chris isn't preparing for a race, may get one.

Heads turn whenever an engine growls to life at Lime Rock, but when a Seven burbles everyone pays attention; it stands out even among these odd, noisy cars. People grin appreciatively as the roadster *gar-gar-gar*s by, and sometimes you hear them sorting out its singular charm. Her: *Now that's a great old car.* Him: *But look, it's new!*

The Seven I drove at Lime Rock was a 1989 model built by a Seven & Elans customer. Chris introduced us, and David mentioned casually that his car was in the flea-market section of the track. Would I be interested in a ride? He didn't have to ask twice.

David's Seven was black, and customized. Nothing, to be sure, like the look-at-me Sevens I'd seen in books, which sported T-frame hardtops and boat-tail rear ends; no, David's modifications were practical, because he raced his Seven in autocrosses and drove it to work eleven months a year. He'd added a sump pump, to ensure oil delivery during hard cornering; a choke, good for the winter but sufficiently fiddly (to use the English vernacular) that Chris recommends against them; and a removable tool box mounted on top of the heater. He also installed stone guards on the rear fenders— not Caterham's steel shields but trimmed rubber mats, an inelegant addition for which Chris surely gave him grief. David's got more grief in store, too, if he ever devises the acrylic, gull-wing top I've heard him talk about. Imagine touring country roads in winter while hunkered down in a cozy, see-through Seven—it'd be spectacular, the modern equivalent of a sleigh ride . . . if you could get any traction in the snow.

The scenery around Lime Rock is beautiful all year, and

surprisingly unspoiled by the racetrack's proximity. The commercial buildup is minimal and restrained, and you can drive a few hundred yards from the course without noticing it. The one giveaway, as at the Caterham works, is the exotic vehicles nearby. Once, at the state-highway turnoff, I saw a race-car trailer towed by a hearse—driven, I assume, by a fatalistic competitor.

Once through the track's infield gate, top down of course, David and I were in a green cathedral. The Seven poured out hydrocarbons and carbon monoxide, yes, but it still seemed to amplify, not abridge, our connection to nature. Weren't roads like this made for cars like this? The Seven almost disappeared from consciousness in the sensory rush of air and light and color—though I could certainly hear the car. David's commentary was almost impossible to catch above the constant carburetor blat.

"The wipers didn't work (*buuuuuuuuurrrr*—steady cruising) for months (*uuuuuuuuuuuhhhhhhh*—corner deceleration) until they suddenly started up at Easter (*whiiiiiiiiiinnnn*—back up to 4,500 rpm). It was a miracle."

David was showing me what the Seven could do, taking curves cleanly at forty-five miles an hour that a sedan wouldn't like at twenty-five. The ride was stiff, the car jouncing at every bump and dip in the asphalt, but you usually registered them in time to brace yourself: Indeed, you couldn't avoid seeing the ups and downs—because the car was so close to the road, and because being in the Seven heightened your perceptions manyfold. You felt incredibly vulnerable, no question, but your greatest fear was not bodily injury but missing something. The Seven promised unrepeatable experience; it insisted you pay attention, seize the day.

At first, accounting for the root-plagued street, David drove (in Seven terms) sedately. But when we turned onto a wider road he stretched the car, taking it to fifty-five and nearly ripping the baseball cap off my head; I had to rebutton it to painful tightness. (Contact-lens wearers are advised to use goggles, for above 70 mph the lenses may be sucked from their eyes.) A few minutes later David pulled over, and when the road was empty suggested I get ready to feel some power.

"It's not such a thrill for me anymore," he said, almost apologetically. "It's the road-holding that makes the car. But people get a kick out of the acceleration."

He looked up and down the highway, revved the engine, let out the clutch, dropped the gas pedal, and . . .

I should give up, in truth, for it's impossible to do justice to the first-timer's experience. Nonetheless:

The tires screeched, the seat collided with my back, and the pavement, an arm's length away, came and went at an alarming rate. The Seven drove straight but seemed to go slightly left or right many times a second: Every imperfection in the asphalt deflected the car a bit, and every bump the tires experienced we experienced, too. The tach read 6,000 rpm in an instant; the carbs shrieked, the car hurtled, and David slashed the shift back to second.

A millisecond of calm as the revs dropped, but only the calm before the storm; the Seven leaped forward again, the road now feeling like a runway. David upshifted to third, and when we returned to 4,000 rpm, a moment later, said "That's sixty." We hit seventy-five in fourth, took a turn at speed that pushed me hard into the side of the car, flew up to eighty-five as David tromped the accelerator coming out of the turn and stair-stepped into fifth. We reached ninety, almost, before David let the Seven coast down to fifty-five, a BMW once miles ahead now within hailing distance.

The demonstration couldn't have lasted thirty seconds but seemed much longer. I felt the foolish grin on my face, the tingle of windburn on my cheeks, the buzz of fresh noise in my ears.

David pulled over a second time and said, nonchalantly, "Wanna drive?"

Already shell-shocked from the bulletlike acceleration, now I was dumbfounded, too. But I could hardly decline; how demanding could the Seven be if an owner allowed a virtual stranger behind the wheel? David must be naive, lucky, suicidal—either that, or an average driver can handle the car.

I'm not sure what expectations I had for the Seven, but the car easily surpassed them. Driving it was effortless: The steering was extraordinarily responsive, the Seven going precisely where you pointed it—so precisely, in fact, that for the first minute or so I was incessantly correcting, and overcorrecting, the wheel. The acceleration was equally predictable: The car shot ahead the instant you stepped on the gas, with no delay whatsoever, and took off at a frightening rate only at higher rpms. I assimilated the Seven's manner within five minutes, but never went above forty or into fourth gear. I was totally convinced, though, that the car would do whatever I asked . . . and that I'd better be a good enough driver to know how much I *could* ask.

While returning to the track, me back in the passenger's seat, David said my Seven probably wouldn't drive well until the odometer passed two thousand miles. Indeed, David continued, he'd been disappointed in the car for months after completing it; he thought he'd made a terrible mistake, because the acceleration was flat in spots, the engine sometimes balky. Once broken in, though, the Seven displayed its true nature, and David became a True Believer.

As I slid into my on-its-last-legs Subaru, I decided I could live with such problems. They were, after all, familiar.

10

JUMPING THE TRACKS

Like Taylor and Gilbreth and Ford, I too am a devotee of efficiency and economy (read, *tightfistedness*). So it made sense to tour the Caterham works and Portmeirion—the Welsh holiday resort where *The Prisoner* was filmed—on the same trip to Britain. But that didn't happen, because friends, living in London the summer before I took delivery of the Seven, invited us over for a family visit. The offer was too good to pass up; Thea was young enough to fly free and could hang out with Lisa and Mary while I borrowed Marsden's Passat to run down to Caterham.

No doubt we could have managed a quick expedition to The Village, but I wanted to be there during a "Portmeiricon" (as it's called), the annual convention of the main *Prisoner* fan club. I pictured myself arriving at the

"Six of One" gathering in a borrowed Seven; by then I was a book columnist for the *Los Angeles Times* and thought Caterham would loan me a car if southern California publicity seemed possible.

In the end, though, I chickened out. A Caterham-subsidized trip would have been journalistically unethical, for one thing, but more to the point, I wasn't sure I could handle a Seven on its home turf. By then I had driven 1) a Seven, 2) in London traffic, 3) on the "wrong" side of the road, and 4) a right-hand-drive, left-hand-gearshift automobile—but never all four at the same time. The more I thought about the trip, the less confident I became about completing the four-hundred-mile Portmeirion–Dartford circuit in one piece . . . especially since I'd broken the Passat's passenger-side mirror, in a too-close encounter with another vehicle, just minutes from Caterham.

When the time came, consequently, I took The Train to The Village. Les was in London once more, so I stopped for a couple days beforehand to sleep on Mrs. Forsythe's library floor and gorge on whole-wheat waffles.

I had visited Portmeirion years earlier, fascinated not only by *The Prisoner* but the place itself. The resort's creator, the iconoclastic architect Sir Clough Williams-Ellis, called it "my home for fallen buildings," and so it is: an Italianate village reconstituted from scores of interesting structures shipped here from all over the world (though mostly Europe). Williams-Ellis approached architecture the way Chapman approached engineering: buying old, undervalued ingredients—in the Welshman's case, bell towers, cupolas, terraces, archways, lintels, facades, grottoes—and adapting them to new functions. Like Chapman, Williams-Ellis had a genius for revision, transfiguring found objects so completely that their original functions were forgotten.

Lewis Mumford called Portmeirion "a folly," "a deliberately irresponsible reaction" to modern architecture. And there's no arguing with that assessment; the place is all surface, all show—an impression heightened by the frequent use of pastel paints and tromp l'oeil effects. No wonder Portmeirion reminded McGoohan of a contemporary hell; genuinely attractive, and seemingly authentic, it is in reality quite false, just like the replicated "home" in which Number Six resides.

Portmeirion, moreover, is a natural contradiction. Witness sunsets over the water, the masses of blooming rhododendrons, the emerald green hills across Tremadoc Bay, and the resort seems an idyll: You can see why Noel Coward wrote *Blithe Spirit* here (in seven days). But consider the rugged mountains behind Portmeirion, its coastal isolation, the stone boat cemented to the main hotel's dock . . . and the place becomes, with a slight change of tone or allegiance, a prison. (You don't suppose Aldous Huxley, reportedly a Portmeirion guest at least once, conceived *Brave New World* here?) From my quarters, on the top floor of a three-story cottage called The Anchor, I could see the mudflats of the Traeth Bach estuary; it was impossible to look on them without thinking of Stephen Dedalus's meditations on Sandymount strand, just across the Irish Sea.

The Six of One convention, for many people, is a form of therapy. Attendees come from many different countries but are drawn for similar reasons: a sense of alienation, of threatened individuality. At the Portmeiricon they both address and live out their fears, discussing the meaning of *The Prisoner* while wearing, simultaneously, its signature attire—white-piped jackets and straw boaters, colorful striped capes and matching umbrellas, lapel pins reading "Questions are a burden to others: answers a prison for oneself." Village Radio, in the meantime, broadcasts trivial announcements in a soothing, Pollyanna voice: "Good morning, good morning! Isn't it a lovely day!"

My assigned roommate was Ted, a Six of One veteran who had been organizing and attending Portmeiricons for more than a decade. He seemed to know everyone, which gave me the willies; he was too casual and friendly to be mistaken for Number Two, but would have risen to the top, clearly, in the televised Village. Ted always gave familiar faces a tip of the boater, and on parting a "Be seeing you"—the series' barbed good-bye. My roommate knew this annual re-creation was laced with paradox, but regarded the incongruity as part of the fun. "Surely 'tis a little strange," he told me. "A way to haul your intellectual ashes."

A Six of One colleague, Drew, brought the contradiction to life at a bull session for Portmeiricon novices. He asked the fifteen-odd people gathered under the Hercules Gazebo to write down their reasons for identifying with Number Six . . . and we fell for it, to a man and woman.

"Everyone finished?" asked Drew when all heads were raised. "Right. Now, why'd you do what I told you to?"

We were a little confused.

"You automatically did what I asked. Why didn't anyone tell me to piss off?"

We understood, then, Drew's point—that people can be sheep. A rapid-fire discussion ensued in which those present, mostly men in their twenties and thirties, cataloged government intrusions on their lives. I felt as if I'd stumbled on a Mensa-hippie survivalist sect.

"They've installed surveillance cameras in Birmingham city center," said a man in a boater. "England's becoming more like The Village every day."

"And that new law," added a younger man in jeans, referring to legislation that had made legally incriminating a suspect's silence. "Incredible—or I wish it were."

"I'm glad I'm taking my family to Australia," said a middle-aged woman. She spoke in disgusted tones, and I didn't doubt that her emigration—she boarded a boat the following month—was political as much as economic.

Another man, a social-service provider, described the red tape that prevented him from accomplishing anything significant for his clients. "It's all a bloody waste," he said.

The anger was palpable. For many in the group *The Prisoner* was a crucible for personal and political indignation, a way of reassuring themselves they weren't alone. That seemed especially true for the teenagers on hand (most of whom arrived with their parents). For them *The Prisoner* was a video version of *Catcher in the Rye*.

"I feel like Number Six all the time," declared one boy, not older than fourteen, with great passion. "And we're all living in The Village; the whole world's a Village where we can't be individuals."

Prisoner fans have heard that idea a thousand times—indeed, one Number Two dreams of a global Village—but many in the gazebo were glad to hear it said with the enthusiasm of new discovery. Some nodded approvingly, but most did not—perhaps a little fearful, in light of Drew's mind game, of going along with the crowd.

One man, though, responded directly. "But we can't *all* be individuals. I want to be, of course, everyone does, but somebody's got to support *me* while I'm doing what I want. Like being here. Maybe we have to take turns being individuals."

The discussion had no resolution, naturally, and ended only with the arrival of giant placards bearing the likeness of Number Six. So began the parade—a re-creation of the election rally in "Free for All," the episode in which Number Six agrees to campaign for Number Two's position at Number Two's personal request. Why does Two ask, and why does Six consent? Number Two sees an opportunity to co-op; Number Six a chance to turn the tables, by using the phony election to foment rebellion. The ploy doesn't work, of course, for anyone: Number Six is in fact elected, but the Villagers ignore him when he announces, at his inauguration, that they are "free to go." He tries to flee himself, but is pursued, beaten, and finally asked, by the newest Number Two—previously his campaign assistant—"Will you never learn?"

The highlight of the convention is the re-creation of the opening scene from "Checkmate." A giant chess board is laid out on Portmeirion's main lawn, not far from Number Six's lodgings, and here the Villagers/prisoners play knights and bishops as well as pawns. Number Six, asked conspiratorially to play the white queen's pawn, stumbles on a cell of dissidents; one, the queen's rook, makes an unauthorized move and checks the opposing king. An alarum sounds, a police buggy drives up, and the offending rook is carted off to the Village hospital. Number Six asks what will happen to the man, and the queen replies, "He'll be well looked after . . . they'll get the best specialists to treat him."

The re-creation is quite effective, one year even causing injury (when the police jeep hit a spectator). The version I saw was almost as dramatic, though for entirely different reasons: A wedding reception took place in the wings. A former Portmeirion waitress scheduled her marriage, deliberately, for the Six of One weekend, wanting fans of *The Prisoner* to be part of the scene. The bride and groom—who in his youth dropped eels in the hotel pool—stood in the middle of the chessboard for wedding portraits . . . which surely will require, years hence, elaborate explanation. Especially the presence of Number Six; for some shots he was invited to stand alongside the newlyweds.

McGoohan, for whom *The Prisoner* was a protest against mindless herd behavior, has kept his distance from both Six of One and the series itself. You can't blame him: For all its freethinking, anticult messages, *The Prisoner* ended up creating a cult of its own. As cults go, however, it is benign, for even hard-core adherents recognize the series' flaws: the action-adventure and spy-genre conventionality, the cut-and-paste surrealism and silly science fictions, not to mention the dated, TV-budget cheesiness—Rover, most notably, the weather-balloon gatekeeper spawned by the Village's giant Lava Lamp. But the merits of *The Prisoner* far outweigh its failings, for no series of the era had its psychological complexity or ambition. Good and evil seemed to fall, at first, into predictable black-and-white patterns, but viewers who stuck with the program learned that appearances, almost invariably, deceive.

Number Six, portrayed throughout the series as a heroic moralist, discovers that on a very personal level in the series' final episode, "Fall Out." Having broken down one final Number Two (played by Leo McKern, of "Rumpole" fame) in the regression-to-childhood, duel-to-the-death episode "Once Upon a Time," Number Six himself becomes the new Number Two. His first request, naïvely, is to meet Number One. After a ritual investiture, mock trials, and a small-arms battle fought to the strains of "All You Need Is Love," Number Six tracks down his nemesis, pulls off his white hood, then his monkey mask, and discovers beneath it . . . his own face.

The viewer realizes, then or subsequently, that he's been given the riddle's solution many times before. It's prefigured in the opening sequence of every *Prisoner* episode, when the new Number Two, in response to McGoohan's asking "Who is Number One?", invariably replies "*You* . . . are Number Six." As McGoohan would later explain, with a sensitivity and introspection not commonly associated with the entertainment industry, "The greatest evil that one has to fight constantly, every minute of the day until one dies, is the worser part of oneself."

Before leaving Portmeirion I ducked into the Village gift shop, self-described as the "Prisoner Information Centre" and located in Number Six's television residence. A hand-lettered sign in the window reads

Important! This is an independent shop about *The Prisoner* and nothing else. Warning! People who have not seen *The Prisoner* probably won't understand anything in here.

Shortly after going inside I was followed by the Portmeiricon's Number Six impersonator, who shut the door behind him. Assuming the shop was about to close, I opened the door again and walked out . . . to the clicking and flashing of cameras and a tour guide muttering about an "unexpected exit." I had mistakenly interrupted yet another Six of One re-creation . . . and so have been immortalized in a handful of vacation albums as "the jerk who spoiled the shot—he's supposed to be Number Six."

If I learned one thing in law school, it's that you may have to read a paragraph—even a sentence—three, five, ten times before claiming to understand it. Language is slippery, and so is authorial intent, not to mention received interpretation; the *aha!* moment is often the very point at which you start going astray. The meaning of a text is constantly in flux, varying with the times and with the reader, so you must always be prepared to reevaluate your views. The constellations in your schoolbook aren't the only arrangements of the night sky, and may hide deeper, more resonant configurations.

I read scores of books while building the Seven, following references and quotations in myriad directions, and the least promising often proved the most interesting. I knew what I'd be getting, more or less, upon rereading *Howard's End* and *A Passage to India*; both deal wonderfully and unpredictably with cultural clashes, with the yawning divide of difference. The scientist/novelist C. P. Snow—who once spent a weekend at my grandmother's house, her second husband (and her third, for that matter, after her second widowing) having been chairman of UC Berkeley's English department—addressed the same theme in *The Two Cultures*. There he deplored the growing estrangement and credibility gap between the arts and the sciences.

I hit pay dirt in *The Structure of Scientific Revolutions*. I had encountered the book only tangentially in college, and only as an historical marker: By the 1970s it was platitudinous to say that science was neither progressive nor objective. While reading the late Thomas Kuhn's unglossed argument, however, I discovered his thinking ran more broadly, and much more deeply, than conventional paraphrases imply. The phenomenon was becoming annoyingly, intriguingly familiar: a book I first met in young adulthood demonstrating its significance, and often a new, divergent inflection, only when I reread it years later. I couldn't help wondering: *Had my higher education been, well, not so high?*

I picked up *Structure*, after running across it in a used bookstore, because I had read somewhere that Kuhn highlighted the double-edged nature of professionalism. Expertise could blind as well as enlighten, he was said to argue—and so he did, in ways more profound than that oversimplification indicates.

Kuhn ventured, in a nutshell, that science evolves toward objective truth not cumulatively and directly but through a succession of theories, new ones emerging when flaws in the old become too obvious to ignore. And it doesn't evolve gracefully, either; most scientific research, Kuhn wrote, is "a strenuous and devoted attempt to force nature into the conceptual boxes supplied by professional education." Science, as a result, "often suppresses fundamental novelties because they are necessarily subversive of its basic commitments."

Kuhn sounds radical, even arrogant, in these passages, but read in context he's the soul of reasonableness. He understands, for one thing, the power of words: He employs *revolution*

in the book's title, not evolution, in part because the latter is wrongly joined at the hip to the idea of "progress" . . . and Kuhn isn't convinced that science, let alone history, climbs ever upward toward majesty. (Will man seem an advanced species should a nuclear holocaust, or a lab-made virus, leave the earth dominated by cockroaches, sharks, and microbes?) Neither does Kuhn repudiate science's "conceptual boxes"; he recognizes their importance as building blocks, but also that they can screen, blinker, narrow one's vision. Scaffolding may be essential to the creation of physical or mental architecture but should not be mistaken for substance, nor obstruct conflicting perspectives.

The key word in Kuhn's book is "paradigm," and it has come to be defined—when not casually misinterpreted, which it usually is—as an intellectual framework. The paradigm need not be fully rational, nor even readily apparent to its adherents: Indeed, murkiness and ill-definition are crucial ingredients of a paradigm, for raggedness—the ability to be many things to many people—allows a paradigm to embrace and delimit a culture, umbrella-like, that would otherwise scatter in the wind. The acquisition of a paradigm, Kuhn wrote, signals a field's maturity: that certain principles are shared by group members without question, without reserve.

My class, back in high school, had a designated paradigm questioner. We didn't know it at the time, of course: Gar was very smart and a good friend—for a while he too hung out with me and Les and Hugh—but sometimes brought up issues so elementary they drew exasperated looks from students and teachers alike. Only in retrospect, I regret to say, did I realize Gar was doing our dirty work, posing baseline questions that should have been on everyone's mind. In biology, physics, precalculus, history—every few months Gar would raise his hand and say, "I don't understand that. Why?" The teacher, after a follow-up "But *why*?" or two from Gar, would move on, frequently oblivious that the ground had shifted, that his cement foundation had been transformed into quicksand.

Gar now lives in Alaska, and *Structure*, provided an explanation. He never found, in the lower forty-eight at least, a way of grounding life that withstood even teenage scrutiny. Gar had to make, or uncover, a paradigm of his own.

I was late to that dance. In high school I wanted to fit in more than find my own path, maybe Gar could resist conformity because he eased naturally into the "in" crowd, being a better athlete, a better doper, a better ladies' man (and I wasn't a slouch at the first two). I trace my need for acceptance to the age of seven (!), when my family left Cambridge for California and my full-bore English accent rendered me, to many people, incomprehensible. For the next few years two of my best friends—one at the top of the class, one toward the bottom—had similar accents, and I'm sure we kept company mostly because we didn't have to repeat ourselves.

I was conscious, even then, of wanting to swim in the mainstream, despite being more comfortable in backwaters and eddies and marginal shallows; with oddballs, dissidents, Number Sixes. And if I wanted to retain my personal history, what better way—excuse me while I slip into another metaphor—to join the main road than in a Seven? That contradiction in terms, that paradigm buster, that near-living fossil; the one car that's in the world but not quite of it. What the hell, let's change metaphors once more: I'm a train that couldn't find himself until he jumped the tracks.

11

QUALITY FAILURE

Your life, according to legend, flashes before you at the moment of death, when there's nothing you can do but sit back and enjoy the highlights film. My experience installing the diff-prop assembly wasn't exactly analogous, but close enough to be discomforting.

The procedure was straightforward. Slip the prop shaft into the transmission tunnel, raise the diff until it nearly touches the frame, pass an eleven-inch bolt through a diff lug and two chassis-mounted sleeves—voilà, you're done. The differential hangs nicely from the frame, ready for centering and final bolting.

I knew the task would be physically challenging, but it turned out to be emotionally draining as well. I had never pictured myself lying on a garage floor with a fifty-pound auto part balanced on my chest, very concerned that a sonic boom, say, would bring down five hundred pounds of steel on my helpless body.

I'd worked on jacked-up cars many times before, but this experience was like no other. For one thing, I was completely under the Seven, head beneath the De Dion tube and feet below the engine compartment: Only that position gave me decent leverage over the diff-prop assembly. For another, at ground level the Seven resembled no other car: It was pure machine, having no soundproofing, no underbody panels, an extremely modest floorpan, and not a hint of road grime. From this vantage point the Seven seemed airy, bright, positively roomy—mostly because, with scores of components still awaiting installation, I could see the garage roof right through the chassis.

It was a nice place to daydream, in short, . . . until reality intruded. *Those jerry-rigged sawhorses: one inadvertent whack with the diff, or a misplaced leg movement, and* whomp, *I'm pancaked.* Why in God's name did I buy the first pair of jack stands I saw? Even after reading the warning labels: *never* support a car exclusively with stands, *never* set them at different heights. I had done both (the latter, to compensate for a lumpy garage floor).

Lying under the Seven, the differential at my side, I continued to take much-belated stock. *How could I perform some tasks, like hacksawing the diff, so carefully, and approach others in a sleepwalker's daze? Look around: Those jack stands are too small at the top, the crossbeams too narrow; the rear-end stands are too close together, and also too far forward. And I didn't tell Jenny what was happening, so there's no backup if I, if I . . . Well, shit. Shit, shit, shit.*

So what did I do? I wriggled out from under, asked Jenny if I could borrow the Rabbit, drove to a first-rate auto-supply store, bought heavy-duty jack stands, and devised a new, safe way to support the Seven. Right?

Of course not. I stayed put, because a Y-chromosome

gene kicked in; the one compelling men to do stupid things on purpose.

I studied the diff and divined how long I could hold it up, steadily and at the proper angle, before my arms gave out. I appraised the chassis, attempting to locate those sections that would inflict the least injury should the car fall. I glanced at the garage roof and inadvertently confirmed that danger does magnify one's senses, if only for distraction's sake.

Those pipes and planks stored on the roof joists — a nice tableau, wouldn't it make a terrific photorealist painting? And those rivets, right there, anchoring the Seven's skin to the chassis; a primitive technique, but a handsome effect, clean and uniform. Wait—was that a wren trilling? An early warbler? Could it be a . . .

I would have stayed so for days if the winter chill hadn't crept into my bones.

The key to installation, clearly, was squeezing most of my body between the differential and the garage floor. That'd be the easy part: then a little horizontal dancing—snakelike butt-and-shoulder humping, mostly—to center myself under the diff-mount lugs; a good, careful, clean-and-jerk on the diff itself; a mind-over-matter paralysis of the legs (perhaps I should tie my ankles together?); and yes, finally, the diff would be balancing on my chest. I'd be only a breath away, then, from aligning the thing with the chassis's lugs.

I figured I had one shot, possibly two, to raise the diff to the proper height before I lost control. Timing, beyond a doubt, was everything. By arching my back, taking a deep breath, and supporting the diff lengthwise with my left hand, I was pretty sure I could hold it in position long enough for my right hand to push the long bolt—already test-fitted and greased—home.

Breathe in, breathe out. In, out. In—and not out. *Just think: It's a relaxation-assembly combo technique!*

Up went the diff, raised on my lungs. *Good, fine, yes*—until the diff's passage was interrupted, momentarily but scarily, when the breather tube caught on a chassis cross-member. I worked by feel, since the diff blocked all useful views; with my right hand, which also held the mounting bolt, I located the diff lug. It was good and close, just an inch from the appropriate chassis sleeve.

Cue the Mission: Impossible *technical-problem-solving music, when Peter Lupus is tapping circuits between floors.*

I pushed the bolt through the chassis sleeve until it butted the edge of the diff lug. I slowly raised the lug into alignment, trying to prevent my torso from shivering under the back-arch strain. A few misses, *tap, tap, tap,* and then the bolt slid through; more pushing, and the bolt didn't stop until it hit the second chassis sleeve, where a measured hip roll brought it into line. I nudged the bolt through to its head, and when I exhaled the diff was off my chest, suspended like an ornament.

Life was good.

It would be a stretch to say, despite the anxiety, patterned breathing, and substantial weight loss, that installing the diff was like giving birth. I experienced, nonetheless, a kind of postpartum high, which I wanted to share with Jenny over a cup of coffee. Walking toward the back door, though, I noticed for the first time that the Rabbit wasn't in the driveway . . . which meant that Jenny wasn't home, hadn't been all morning. Leaving me to ponder, once more, why I do the (foolhardy, demented) things I do.

The steering column, as previously noted, resembles a curtain rod. That's not quite accurate, though; in truth it looks like *two* curtain rods clamped together, because federal auto-safety law requires that steering columns be collapsible. Adding such a system to a roller-skate car—*Consumer Reports* would rate the Seven "Absolutely Not Acceptable"—might seem to be whistling past the graveyard, but the feature, however primitive, is comparable to those in most modern automobiles.

The lower steering-column rod is a thirty-plus-inch solid metal dowel. One end terminates in splines that slip into a universal joint on the Seven's chassis-mounted steering rack; the other end, viewed head-on, terminates in a half-moon-shaped tenon. The lower rod's tenon fits inside a notched sleeve on the partially hollow upper rod; the sleeve keeps the two rods lined up, and its notch exposes the lower rod's tenon. Transforming the rods into a single unit is a matter of clamping them together, in the notch, with a pair of steel blocks. Increase the overlap between the two rods, before tightening the blocks, and the column barely protrudes into the cockpit; decrease it, and the steering wheel is under the driver's chin.

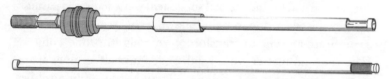

This collapsing-rod system looks rudimentary but is actually quite ingenious. The clamping blocks maintain the rod's length and alignment during ordinary driving conditions, but when the steering wheel is punched with significant force— usually, by the driver's rapidly accelerating body—the upper rod telescopes, to its safe, minimum length, over the lower.

The setup works, too, as I learned one day while moving the wheeled-but-engineless Seven into the garage. The only way to propel and steer the car simultaneously, it seemed, was to push on the steering wheel . . . but after doing so I heard a loud *thunk* and felt the steering wheel bump the dashboard. A few seconds passed before I realized the *oh-my-god-what-have-I-done* sound was not the obliteration of an expensive part but the steering column transforming theory into practice. It had downsized under pressure, just as it was supposed to.

I did obliterate a component, however, while mounting the steering column. It was my first grievous mistake, though not the typical one for this assembly, which is forgetting to install the steering column's sealing plate. (Leave it out and you'll reply like Colin Chapman when asked, after a rainy weekend, how he liked the Lotus Eleven prototype: "It gets a bit choppy round the ankles.") I was more inventive, installing a rubber bushing in the wrong place.

The steering column passes through a tube in the dashboard, and I assumed, for no good reason, that the bushings would be positioned symmetrically within it. The top bushing was a tight fit, and exotic for the breed: It boasted a friction-defying nylon cylinder on its inmost surface, and metal reinforcement inside its vibration-dampening rubber. I got the bushing in, though, after lubrication and (as the manual suggested) some judicious paring.

My mistake came to light following thirty minutes of frustration attempting to transform two rods into one column. The rods, no matter what I did, ended up half an inch apart. Tapping the upper rod with a mallet did little; adding rubber lube did nothing; screwing the steering wheel onto the upper rod, for leverage, and then pushing on the wheel, only fractured the bushing's inner nylon.

Crraaack.

"Shit! Shitshitshitshit*shit*!"

I couldn't figure out what I'd done wrong. Finally, desperate, I returned to the assembly manual. (Do I stop to get directions when lost? Sometimes.) There it was: "Fit the upper bush into the locating tube under the dashboard, noting how the rubber bumps on the bush locate it."

Yes: but locate it where?

Okay, from the beginning. Rubber bumps: I may not know what a pip is, but bumps I can find.

So the tube, somewhere, has a pair of depressions milled into it? Feel around, stroke the tube. Hmmmm. . . .

Christ on a bicycle. Nowhere, the depressions don't exist.

But wait. The tube's been drilled here, I can feel the hole. Is it a bump-sized hole? Yes! Would a bushing bump, positioned there, stay put? Very possibly.

So why doesn't the manual say the bump goes in a fucking hole! Argghhhh!

I grabbed a screwdriver, strode two paces to the work-bench, and stabbed my shop radio in the gut.

It cost five bucks. I wasn't conscious of extracurricular motivations when buying the radio, but I must have known I'd eventually need to destroy something mechanical when the going got rough. What better than a cheap radio? Especially since it received only a single station, and that one badly?

But here's the strange thing. I realized, as soon as I pulled the screwdriver from the poor bleeding radio, why it didn't work. The tuning pointer didn't move when you twisted the tuning knob: a mechanical problem, and very likely curable. Had the tuning string, which I knew about from my stereo-building days, caught on something? Been inadvertently glued to the case during the radio's construction? On an assembly line, no doubt . . .

I stuck the screwdriver into the radio once more, now aiming where the case and faceplate lapped. I swung the blade in a 180-degree arc. This time, when I pulled the screwdriver out, the tuning pointer moved . . . and the radio came to life (no, I hadn't unplugged it). Soon I was listening to "Car Talk" and pondering a little-known corollary to the law of conservation of energy: for every breakage there is a repair.

The broken bushing was wedged quite securely in the dashboard tube, and to get it out I had to apply some unorthodox, indeed embarrassing, retrieval techniques. Suffice it to say I employed a child's garden rake; two kinds of Peg-Board hooks; needle-nose pliers; vise-grip pliers; a fork with two tines bent into hooks; a stick; a broken stick, accidentally derived from the previous implement; and the upper steering rod itself. Eventually the bushing popped out, distorted beyond recognition

And here's the big question. When Chris Tchórznicki reads this list, will he laugh or cry?

Kit-car builders are shadowed by error and calamity. So many things to go wrong; so many parts to disappear; so many unexpected problems, so many new roadblocks. For all that, though, I was in a much better position than most automobile do-it-yourselfers, since I'd purchased an everything-but-the-kitchen-sink kit from a single, reputable supplier, and also had Chris to lean on. But I could screw up nonetheless, as the steering column proved.

Until then I had never really considered failure, that I might never complete the Seven. Mostly, I guess, because the build didn't take great talent or dedication, and because fatal mistakes—to the car at least—were almost impossible to make. But the bushing debacle created a distinct paranoia, for it revealed how easily you could build failure into the car. Forget to lubricate the steering column; ignore a defective bushing; overtighten the safety/adjustment blocks—things might look fine, and feel fine, for hundreds of road miles . . . and then the steering wheel jams as you take a lovely 25-mph turn at 50. The Seven's wrapped around a tree, and you're dead.

That's why Caterham advises a postbuild inspection. The cars are fine, usually, but Chris mentioned one Seven in which the lower steering rod wasn't properly seated in the steering rack's U-joint. The builder was lucky to make it to the inspection in one piece, for with only a quarter-inch overlap between the rod and the joint, a bad bump could have uncoupled the parts and given new meaning to the term "understeer." Without the inspection—and if the builder himself didn't catch the foul-up—he would have had a serious accident.

Chris delivered that cautionary tale, and the following week a replacement bushing, when I confessed my steering-assembly sin. (Soon after the substitute arrived, be it noted, I had two bushings in the hand.) Chris intended the story as a warning, and that's how I took it—but also as a parable of mid-century Detroit.

Defective vehicles surely rolled off Henry Ford's assembly lines, but imagine how many more emerged from Alfred Sloan's. General Motors' cars were compromised from the get-go; with the company expressly favoring both style and profitability over engineering, the quality of the cars couldn't help but suffer. That didn't become fully apparent until the 1970s, of course, when European and Japanese manufacturers demonstrated that Fordism's automotive goals—efficiency, reliability, economy—were timeless. Sloan had built failure into his cars—that was the beating heart of "planned obsolescence"—and everyone in the United States paid the price. As numerous statistics attest, when Detroit sneezes, the nation catches cold.

In 1950, more than 75 percent of all motor vehicles sold worldwide were made by American companies; by 1982 the figure was less than 20 percent. The decline is astoundingly steep, and with one in six U.S. jobs related in some way to the automobile, had an enormous impact. Billions of dollars went overseas, hundreds of thousands of workers lost their jobs, and Sloanism became regarded in many quarters as a kind of disease. Sloan's successor, "Engine Charlie" Wilson, created only a minor stink when he said, in 1953, "For years I thought what was good for our country was good for General Motors, and vice versa. The difference did not exist. Our company is too big"; twenty years later the quotation (badly abbreviated) represented corporate arrogance at its worst. Locked in a passionate embrace with fashion and marketing, sales and share, Detroit had forgotten that the automobile was, above all, transportation.

And it could only blame itself, for Detroit long ignored the one man determined to return mass-manufacturing to its roots. W. Edwards Deming was an odd combination of Ford, Leland, Taylor, and Gilbreth: a management consultant who believed in engineers, a statistician who disliked conventional categories, a lover of efficiency who loved quality even more. (You don't suppose Robert Pirsig, whose transcendent goal in *Zen and the Art*. . . was a supercharged "Quality," had read his work?) Deming tried to interest U.S. manufacturers in his throw-out-the-rule-book theories, but only in Japan did he find an appreciative audience. He was influential there as early as 1950, preaching continuous improvement, dedication to the product, and teamwork, but simultaneously spurned in the United States. "Total Quality Management" sounds like an all-American buzz phrase, but—like the cars it first inspired—TQM is also a Japanese import, returning across the Pacific to save an industry that had been too busy digging its own grave, years earlier, to heed its offspring.

If Detroit's automakers had listened to Deming, they wouldn't have been forced to play catch-up. In the 1960s they would have built cars as reliable as the VW Beetle, having recognized the student's need for an inexpensive car, the urbanite's for a small car. In the 1970s GM wouldn't have built the Vega, whose aluminum engine tended to burn out, or Ford the Pinto, in which some sixty people died because of management's reluctance to install a nine-dollar gas-tank safety device. For more than a decade Detroit did little but flounder, unable to comprehend that its basic problem lay not with the line workers—so easy to blame, those blue collars!—but with executive mismanagement. Robotics and automation and greater control wasn't the answer, as Detroit assumed; it needed, instead, to watch, listen, let go.

And belatedly, slowly, Detroit did learn from its mistakes. Of the five cars I owned in my first twenty-two years of driving, none were born in the U.S.A.; the two cars I own today—all three, if you include the Seven—are American-made. Detroit realized, finally, that Henry Ford was more often right than wrong . . . and even right about *being* wrong. It's not a famous Ford quote, but one of his best: "Failure is only the opportunity more intelligently to begin again."

12

LEARNING TO FISH

We were in London's National Gallery, or possibly the Tate, gazing upon a social satire—I forget which—by William Hogarth. Most everyone in the room was a British Studies major, an interdisciplinary program in which students examined culture through a variety of overlapping lenses—history, art, literature, economics, and so on. Hogarth was an appropriate figure to explore because his work broke boundaries; although he could paint flattering portraits and landscapes, Hogarth was more interested in capturing aspects of England considered, then, outside the pale. Rather than exploit an easy talent for oils and lead, he elevated the low-brow art of social commentary by reimagining it.

The speaker, a distinguished Yale professor, was

describing Hogarth's relationship to Gin Lane culture when a student raised her hand. I don't remember the question, but the answer was a longish, slightly exasperated disquisition on the limits of, and opportunities provided by, the British Studies program. The professor was sympathetic toward interdisciplinary studies, since he taught in both the art and English departments, but wanted to impress upon us that outside-the-box thinking required singular intellectual rigor. British Studies majors were expected to master every relevant discipline on its own terms, he implied, not pick and choose among them—to dip a toe in art history here, or literature there, as circumstances warranted.

"You must not," he thundered, so far as that's possible in a museum, "be dilettantes!"

Gar came to mind. *But why?*

I wish I knew then what I know now, for I might have worked up the nerve to defend amateurism. Weren't we spending most of our time studying dilettantes: the gentleman architects, the closeted woman novelists, the aristocratic poets, the society painters, the wide-ranging men of letters? And if British Studies was to become a respectable field, didn't it need to develop, as Thomas Kuhn suggested, its own methods, its own priorities and principles and paradigm? Besides, what the hell's wrong—sorry, professor—with studying something merely for the love of it? Why should amateurism (from the Latin *amor*) or dilettantism (from the Italian *dilettare*, to delight) be regarded with disparagement, provoke such contempt?

But I didn't say anything. A few years later the British Studies major vanished from the Yale campus, if not from the catalogue (a few courses are still offered at the university's Paul Mellon Centre in London); the program's allegiances were too thin and diffuse to generate a power base. Lacking an obvious ideology or jargon, the program drew neither publicity nor enthusiastic adherents, and was soon pushed even farther to the side by fields like ethnic and gender and cultural studies, by methodologies like deconstruction and multiculturalism. Strange but predictable; when people talk about breaking barriers, "thinking outside the box," what they usually want is for the listener to climb into *their* box.

Every once in a while you run across a reference to the last individual to "know everything." It's almost a joke, but not quite: As late as two hundred, three hundred years ago a dedicated reader could, conceivably, absorb and comprehend almost everything important then known to man. That reader didn't work, of course: or rather, becoming educated *was* his work, which he would in turn—like encyclopedist Denis Diderot, or dictionary makers Samuel Johnson and Noah Webster—share with others. Citing Webster is a stretch, since he lived into the 1840s, but I can't resist the reference because he's yet another ancestor. Julia Webster, his daughter, was my great-great-great-grandmother, having married Chauncey A. Goodrich (who, after turning down the presidency of Williams College, helped his father-in-law revise the dictionary).

I come by my bookishness naturally, in other words, by way of genetics if nothing else. And that's a problem in the Information Age, for my hereditary aversion to ignorance is quaint, obsolete; where does the dyed-in-the-wool generalist, the committed jack-of-all-trades, go to work? He must, it seems, create his own job. I think of Les: scholar, mechanic, translator, teacher, computer programmer, scavenger, nomad. Of Weil: philosopher, theologian, labor organizer, journalist, soldier, mystic. Of Thoreau, self-described in a letter to his Harvard class secretary (1837): "a Schoolmaster—a Private Tutor, a Surveyor—a Gardener, a Farmer—a Painter, I mean a House Painter, a Carpenter, a Mason, a Day-Laborer, a Pencil-Maker, a Glass-paper Maker, a Writer, and sometimes a Poetaster." I could say much the same, only it isn't socially acceptable.

And where does that leave me? In search of a working niche that isn't narrow; a way of reading experience undistorted by theory, by wishfulness, by financial over- or undercompensation. Such employment has proved difficult to find, for stay in a job long enough and you discover, eventually, that the professional lens you've adopted can act like a funhouse mirror. To the point, sometimes, that you take wavy caricature for reality.

No one has expressed that idea more eloquently than Mark Twain—printer, prospector, journalist, novelist, lecturer, failed businessman, and riverboat captain. "Now when I had mastered the language of this water," he wrote in *Life on the Mississippi*, describing this last-named employment,

> . . . I had made a valuable acquisition. But I had lost something, too. I had lost something which could never be restored to me while I lived. All the grace, the beauty, the poetry had gone out of the majestic river! . . .
>
> All the value any feature of it had for me now was the amount of usefulness it could furnish toward compassing the safe piloting of a steamboat. Since those days I have pitied doctors from my heart. What does the lovely flush in a beauty's cheek mean to a doctor but a "break" that ripples above some deadly disease?. . . [D]oesn't he sometimes wonder whether he has gained most or lost most by learning his trade?

Loss—that's what I felt in my bones. That becoming specialized, professionalized, was falling down a mineshaft, never to see natural daylight again. The descent might prove rewarding, in gold and experience, but the personal costs were high, too high for me.

Teach a man to fish, goes the Chinese proverb, and you bestow the paramount gift of self-sufficiency. Now, though, we endorse dependency, dress ourselves in fashionable blinkers, remain comfortably ignorant of most every skill other than our (specialized) own. Some unknown *they* does the fishing for us . . . and we never learn the taste of fresh trout, because we never make the cast ourselves, never experience the craft.

Lotus Ltd., in the early days, staged "world record" attempts at Seven building in order to demonstrate its easiness. The fastest time, set in 1968, was four hours—an astonishing feat, even though many kit Sevens of that era were shipped in more complete form. Lotus failed to note, of course, that the builder, a company employee, had previously assembled and disassembled the very same "world-record" car to ensure a fast and perfect fit. Lotus kept the build time just this side of implausible, it's said, by insisting the builder take numerous tea breaks.

Present-day customers are told they can get the Seven on the road in sixty hours, and some people have done just that. It's unusual, though, for most Seven builders find their labor hours dwarfed by those spent sitting around, tapping their feet, awaiting the arrival of missing parts. That occurred in my case, certainly: The only reason I installed the steering column relatively early in the build was because I didn't have on hand components essential to completing the wheel assemblies.

I couldn't finish the rear-axle assembly in sequence because I didn't have the bolts that connect the rear hubs to the hub carriers and then to the De Dion tube. The bolts had to be installed and tightened before the brakes went on, and I wasn't about to buy replacements locally because the manual specified heavy-duty, high-tensile bolts designed for "safety critical" applications. And I couldn't finish the front end, either, because the "nylocs" were missing—the nuts with nylon inserts that connect the steering track-rods to the front uprights. The nylon in nylocs, interestingly, acts in the opposite way as its cousin in the steering-column bushing. While the bushing nylon promotes slipperiness, the nylocs' inserts create friction—the bolt threads cut into the nylon as they're turned, and so trap themselves as you twist the bolt head.

Missing parts like these wrought havoc with my build schedule. I'd arrive in Hastings bright and early and full of enthusiasm, only to discover the work I'd planned couldn't be done—with the result that I commenced other projects for which I wasn't prepared. I'd start on what seemed a straightforward task, only to discover I hadn't understood the reasoning behind a part's placement, the performance goal behind an engineering decision.

Bolting the seat-belt reels into their wheel-well niches, for example, should have been a simple chore. But I couldn't find the correct lockwashers, so I substituted slightly thicker ones. How much difference could a single millimeter make? Plenty (as that old Benson & Hedges cigarette ad forever reminds us): The thicker lockwashers allowed the bolt to protrude just enough to threaten the damper units. Under hard braking the springs might touch the bolt ends, and that wasn't good. The Pinto embodied this problem at its worst; the car tended to explode into flames during rear-end accidents because unnecessary bolt ends on its differential opened the gas tank like "can openers" (as one plaintiff's lawyer put it).

Off with the damper units, off with the seat-belt reels. Back on again, once I'd located the proper lockwashers. Off with everything yet again, when I realized the rear antiroll bar was fastened by bolts that would become inaccessible once the seat-belt reels were installed. (The manual caused this error, picturing the bar's anchors as integral studs rather than bolts.) By afternoon's end I felt like the antimatter equivalent of Jack, the house builder: This is the bar that requires a stud that secures the reel that needs an anchor that lacks the washer that grips the bolt that rubs the spring that encircles the damper that I shouldn't have installed today, regardless.

The upshot of this assembly-disassembly routine was mostly skinned knuckles. The blood was faintly gratifying, however, for in some adolescent way it forced me to take inventory (emotional, if not material). Pain does concentrate the mind; prompts important questions like *How could I be so stupid?*

You don't want to ask that very often, of course, but I had to the following day as well, after causing more body damage performing a task I could have done earlier and easier.

When Chris suggested, months previously, that I fill the diff with gear oil before installing it, I dismissed the idea at once. The oil would spill when I attached the diff, or when I removed the shipping covers on the driveshaft openings; and anyway, it'd be a cinch to add the oil later, right? Yes, indeed . . . if you're a whiz at giving differentials IV drips through a puny plastic hose.

The good news was that I had tubing on hand; the bad news was that it resembled a mosquito's proboscis more than an elephant's. I knew I'd made a mistake as soon as I started the drip feed—the flow was only marginally better than *plink plink plink*, but I figured I should suffer for my stupidity. The diff filled to the proper level in fifty minutes . . . which I passed kneeling in a third-rate, freeze-tag Statue of Liberty stance, one hand holding the oil bottle above my head, the other maintaining the seal between bottle and tubing.

Force-feeding the diff was kind of fun, regardless. I thought about the neighbors, who surely wondered why I was building a car in near freezing weather; I listened to the crows, who probably wondered the same thing. And I watched the lubricant ooze, learning that even fresh oil can be adulterated—hundreds of particles floated in the sherry-colored liquid, dandruff, perhaps, from a long-dead dinosaur. The one thing I tried not to think about was my back: When I finally stood up I couldn't manage anything straighter than Dr. Frankenstein's Igor. I resolved in future to follow Chris's instructions to the letter . . . though knowing full well the vow would last only as long as my physical pain.

An incontrovertible sign of spring, for those who work in unheated garages, is the consistency of hand-cleaning lotion changing from Crisco-like to yogurt. Frozen noses and cramped fingers are things of the past; finally you can skip the coveralls, can enjoy mild weather and fresh air (since the garage door is open now, except when it rains). For many Seven builders, though, the warming trend is also a rebuke—a reminder that you're not mechanically ready for the wind-in-the-hair, sun-on-the-face thrills of the driving season.

The disassembly process continued. I had to remove the rear hubs, when I realized the bolts coupling them to the brake discs didn't call for washers. I should have known better: These bolts, unlike those on the front end, bore uncommonly thin heads, which you'd use if clearance was an issue. The mystery wasn't cleared up until I saw that the gigantic nuts—41 mm—securing the rear hubs to the driveshafts would be torqued, eventually, to two hundred pounds. That level of compression would eliminate any conceivable clearance within the unit, and would make designing the assembly's parts rather tricky.

The trouble was, I had not only installed the wrong bolts but—oops—Loctited them. Their extraction was a daunting proposition, consequently, as I feared I'd soon have to buy and wield a blowtorch. In the event, though, the operation was anticlimactic, for the bolts turned with only slightly elevated pressure on the socket wrench—which was both a relief and a disappointment, considering what Loctite is supposed to do. And shouldn't do, as well: A warning on the label says Loctite contains a chemical "known to the State of California to cause cancer." *Hmmmmm: If repeat customers give out before the threadlocker itself, think of the exponential sales boost you'd unleash by marketing Loctite with a lifetime warranty. . . .*

The one benefit of these disassemblies, oddly, was a growing confidence. I began to feel like a veteran Seven builder, for I knew at a glance which parts went where, which bolts, which nuts, which washers—and also where to place tools and components to ease the subsequent reassembly. *Move the driveshaft forward a couple inches and I'll have more wiggle room; raise the jack stands a notch, bingo, more clearance; shift and turn the work light, just so—look, better illumination, better wrench angles.* Repetitive toil is the bane of modern auto assembly, but here I could learn from my failures, transform mistakes into knowledge. As I read, somewhere, during law school, good judgment is bad judgment leavened by experience.

The one new part I installed around this time was the rear antiroll system, and the bar proved a bear. The rear end had gotten crowded—was there *room* for more equipment?—but ultimately the bar went in, connected to the De Dion tube by way of drop links (adjustable rods with ball joints at either end) and to the chassis by aluminum blocks and rubber bushings. The clearance between the antiroll bar and the differential was minimal, but that didn't matter; you could tell, from the bar's pivot points, that the bar would touch the diff only during a forceful accident.

The major suspension task remaining was the installation of the De Dion tube. I had already put in the rear damper assemblies, which locate the tube vertically; now I had to attach the two radius arms, which locate the tube front-to-back, and the A-frame, which locates it side-to-side. Securing the De Dion tube along its x-, y-, and z-axes made it clear why even old-fashioned Caterham designs parts with a computer. Getting the angles exactly right, in three dimensions yet, must have been a hit-and-miss process before CAD/CAM.

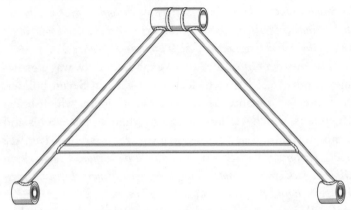

These installations were elementary, though I still had to decide where to attach the Z-arms into the better-handling bolt holes, or the softer-ride pair. I was amazed, at first, to be presented with a choice, but soon realized the selection was essentially between racing and nonracing. Since the Seven is an exceptionally responsive car right out of the box, literally, you'd select the better-handling position only if you planned to race—unless, of course, you enjoy having your bones jarred.

I also had to figure out how many spacing washers to slip onto the main A-frame bolt in order to center the frame. The total could have been zero or as many as six, which tells you the Seven's chassis components aren't mass-produced. I found that strangely reassuring; the singularity of every part meant you must pay attention while hanging them on the chassis, that you can't work on automatic pilot. Some Seven builders still seem to, of course: so many Z-arms and A-frames have been installed upside down that the mistake is mentioned in the assembly manual.

Although the variations just alluded to ensure that every Seven is unique, I was most impressed, on completing the rear suspension, with how tightly the components worked together. Every moving part nearly grazes everything else; the De Dion tube the differential, the differential the antiroll bar, the antiroll bar the Z-arms, the Z-arms the brake calipers, the brake calipers the dampers, the dampers the De Dion tube. The close tolerances inspire confidence in the Seven's design ... but reduce confidence, simultaneously, in one's ability to consummate that design. The Z-arms, for example, have occasionally been installed not merely upside down but reversed, so they actually hit the brake calipers. At the Caterham factory the gap between idea and execution, theory and practice, is relatively small, but here in Hastings it feels moderately wide. The Seven may be a tiny car, but there's plenty of room to screw up nonetheless.

13

THE COSTS OF CHOICE

The last of the rear-end work was putting in the brake lines. I should have shaped them with a pipe bender, but I didn't, because they looked so easy to fashion by hand. And they were—though my brake lines are in fact an embarrassment, the only aspect of the Seven that truly deserves to be scorned as "amateur." The straight runs aren't quite straight; the turns aren't crisp and regular; and the brake lines wibble and wave where I started a bend prematurely, or had to rebend, or simply got sloppy. I can't explain my cavalier treatment of the Seven's most critical system, but I'll say this—it wasn't due to consummate faith in the emergency brake (see below).

For all that, though, installing the brake lines was a cakewalk compared to bleeding them.

The kit comes with a one-person, bottle-and-tube brake-bleeding apparatus called Eezibleed. Chris Tchórznicki swears by it; I swore at it, though acknowledge, grudgingly, its ingenuity. Brake bleeding ideally calls for three people: one to pump the brake pedal, a second to open and close the bleed valves on each brake, and a third to top off the brake-fluid reservoir (to make sure no air intrudes). The Eezibleed system replaces the pedal-pusher with, of all things, a spare tire; a tube running from the tire to the Eezibleed bottle maintains pressure in the brake lines, thus leaving the mechanic free to go from brake valve to brake valve in search of bubbles and other impurities.

The system didn't work for me, though. Perhaps the tire pressure wasn't high enough; the Seven's sixteen-inch Goodyears (yeah, I know, I know) run at an amazingly low 18 psi. Perhaps the bottle gasket was defective; I never achieved a totally airtight seal. In any case, I did what seemed a reasonable job, finding the brake pedal relatively firm before tossing the Eezibleed bottle in a distant corner of the garage. I subsequently learned, incidentally, that Volkswagen once used a similar system to power a windshield washer. If you ran a hose from the fluid reservoir to a slightly overinflated, front-mounted spare tire, the carmaker found, you could dispense with a washer motor.

I didn't realize how badly I'd fooled myself until more experienced friends came calling.

Mark and Bruce arrived in a 1970s ragtop MGB. Bruce related the familiar story: The car had been sitting in a barn for years, totally neglected, until he bought it for a song and—after various adventures—got the thing running. I should have known, upon hearing the MG's history minutes after my guests' arrival, that I was out of my league.

Mark and Bruce knew their way around cars like I knew my way around English grammar. To that point I had pontificated about the Seven mostly before automobile novices, so it was a shock to find myself talking with people who knew more about my own car—its carburetion, horsepower, suspension, *ad infinitum*—than I did. Sure, I realized Weber carburetors were top of the line, but assumed, until Mark said otherwise, they were German—an awkward misapprehension, considering their cover plates read "Made in Italy" (yes, in English). I felt like a fourth-grader who's been lording superior knowledge over an awestruck second-grader, only to find his status vanish upon the appearance of a teenage brother.

I gave my guests a tour of the Seven. I hadn't planned to put Mark and Bruce to work, but they were champing at the bit to get dirty—indeed, that was half the reason they'd come. And since I harbored misgivings about the car's ability to stop, I was happy to take advantage.

"You guys feel like bleeding brakes?"

They jumped at the chance. Mark climbed behind the wheel, pumped the brake pedal, and announced, "My foot just about went through the firewall."

Shit. Well, better now than later.

Bruce was crouching at the left rear wheel. "Got some brake fluid here. Looks like the valve's not quite closed."

Now why hadn't I noticed that?

Bruce asked for a brake-line wrench, but I had to confess I didn't have one. When he replied "I'll get mine," my embarrassment deepened considerably.

Bruce retrieved a canvas tool roll from the MG and set to work like a car doctor making a garage call. It turned out, to my mortification, that I had bled properly only one or two brake lines. When we finished correcting my mistakes, the system's pressure increased dramatically—you could barely depress the pedal by hand.

The brakes, alas, were the only project on which Mark and Bruce could actively help. Or so it seemed, until Mark picked up some uninstalled parts lying around the garage and automatically explained their function. It was a real education, especially when Mark asked about the clutch system.

The standard Seven, being British, is right-hand drive, so the clutch and its foot pedal are on the same side of the car and connected with an ordinary mechanical linkage. The clutch on the left-hand-drive Seven is catty-corner to the pedal, though, making a hydraulic connection preferable.

I hadn't found the hydraulic-clutch slave cylinder on a previous search, so I told Mark and Bruce the part was AWOL. Then I remembered: The cylinder was used primarily in U.S.-bound Sevens, and I knew I'd unwrapped, nearly a year earlier, a component swaddled in a San Diego newspaper. I ran the part to earth, and Bruce instantly identified the pumplike device as the clutch cylinder. He test-fit it without delay, along with two ancillary parts.

The cylinder's discovery was fortunate as well as fortuitous. These three items—the cylinder, the bolt-and-lock-nut hardware connecting the cylinder to the clutch actuator, and the unit's rubber damper—were illustrated in neither the assembly manual nor the videotape, so I didn't have the faintest idea how to fit them. In a few minutes, though, my automotive betters figured out the only rational way the parts could go together. I might have, too, eventually—but that's doubtful, for Bruce thought the arrangement so intriguing he pulled out a camera and took photographs.

For lunch we adjourned to the local diner, known informally as the Cholesterol Palace, and there I learned the depths of my auto idiocy. Mark made his living as a cranberry farmer but once managed an automotive shop, and had built a gyrocopter from a kit. Bruce was a forest ranger, but was offered a full-time job at a local garage after fixing his Volvo's intractable electrical problem with a borrowed wiring manual. Both Mark and Bruce had stripped engines and rebuilt them;

both talked about auto mechanics as comfortably as they did family pets.

There are amateurs, and rank amateurs, and I knew which class I belonged to. But not, I hoped, for much longer.

Les would have liked Mark and Bruce, and I was sorry he wasn't around to meet them. They too seemed fascinated by everything that crossed their paths, yet also held down respectable, careerlike jobs—something Les had never done, and I had managed for only a few years. To modify a Linus van Pelt one-liner initially referring to *humanity* and *people*, I loved *work*; it was *employment* I couldn't stand.

As a kid I assumed, having read every book by Gerald Durrell, that in adulthood I'd work in a zoo that bred endangered species. I kept that dream for the longest time: As a teenager I was sure I'd become an ethologist, studying animal behavior with Konrad Lorenz. You might think that a high-school summer doing scut work at the local zoo would have dampened my enthusiasm—Gar and I volunteered together, and mostly shoveled shit—but my ardor for animal science didn't flag until college.

I declared myself a biology major right off the bat, and for a few weeks was happy with the decision. Soon, though, I was disheartened by the tone of Bio. 11, its hard-core-science swagger: the hyperrationality, authoritarianism, emphasis on rote learning, and huge numbers of anxious, ambitious, A-crazy premeds (some of whom razored library books, stole class materials, to gain advantage). The lecture class's professor, an ichthyologist immersed in evolutionary development, wanted his students to memorize and reproduce complex diagrams of a cat's eye; I wanted to know why lions sleep so much, how cheetahs run so fast, why house cats hate to swim and jaguars think water's fine.

I felt, despite graduation from a preparatory school,

unprepared for college. In terms of a career, at least; most of the other students, and certainly those from East Coast boarding schools, seemed to have long-term plans for law or medicine or politics or teaching or research. My vision rarely stretched past the following summer; *maybe I'd visit Les in London, take German to be near Cheryl, volunteer at the zoo again.* Something would happen, right, that would tell me what to do?

I waited . . . and waited. And ended up in journalism school, mainly because Berkeley accepted me. Most of my college friends opted for legal education, though few showed much interest in law as undergraduates; as for my closest high-school friends, well, they seemed aimless, too. Gar took off for the boonies; Hugh earned a doctorate but no lasting job; Les continued to drift, acquiring more university credits, cycling around Europe, teaching himself new skills and practicing old ones.

The first couple years out of journalism school I stayed on the margins of the profession. I started working at the *San Francisco Review of Books*, where the fit, for a time, was perfect. The magazine's office was directly above Enrico's coffeehouse, down the street from Carol Doda's strip joint, a block from City Lights bookstore; it was a thrill just working in North Beach, for you never knew what outrageous scenes you might encounter. And not just on the street, either; in our building's dilapidated common area I saw bewigged performers rushing to make the transvestite cabaret show next door, business deals made on a portable phone by a fellow tenant wearing only a bathrobe, marginal Beat poets and significant literary figures in search of bathrooms.

Eventually, though, I needed more. I applied for a job at *California Lawyer*—and was rejected by a Kelly Girl during the initial screening process. A lawyer friend, fortunately, had suggested I send a second application directly to the magazine's editor-in-chief, and that letter got me in the door; she hired me a few weeks later (thus demonstrating the power of both happenstance and friendship). The following week I felt, wearing a tie to work for the very first time, positively bourgeois.

I was inside the system, then, but not for long. Those fishing, fruitless telephone calls; those meetings required by management and policy; those deadlines dictated by printing-plant schedules rather than reportorial comprehension. I rarely had the time, and never the encouragement, to think ideas through, and so took the path of least mental resistance—fell, in other words, into formula. And, eventually, quit the job.

It was in law school, two years later, that I began to appreciate my naïveté. Of course I wasn't happy with standard formulas, arbitrary timetables: They existed to promote convenience, not truth; to maintain the status quo, not improve it. Lawyers knew all this, and so ran most everything—because law was convenience dressed up as truth, the practice of law a juggling of expedient rules. If accepted legal formulas favored your goals, great; if unfavorable, you created a new, hopefully credible formula, and massaged—or misrepresented—the law and the facts to suit.

My constitutional-law professor said it best. Lawyers didn't wait for truth to emerge from a set of facts; they imposed the ring of truth, of plausibility, upon the facts. And if they organized their arguments well—or better than their opponents, at least—their formulas were taken as truths that others, lawyers and nonlawyers alike, had to follow.

I found this thumbnail précis quite dazzling. With one caveat: It valued gloss over reality, said truth was decreed rather than discovered. And decreed by whom, for whom? The client who paid the bills; the metastasizing legal system; the lawyers themselves. Attorneys, by definition, are officers of the court system, but how many spend their lives working for justice?

After a year of law school, and three more trying to figure out why it had gotten so deeply under my skin, I longed for a life less abstract, less involuted, more solid.

I know every nut and bolt and cog. I built it with my own hands.

So maybe it's not surprising I ended up in John's garage.

If you exclude "History is bunk," Henry Ford is most commonly quoted as saying "People can have the Model T in any color—so long as it's black." In fact the T was initially available in six different colors (the other five were red, green, blue, light gray, and dark gray), with black becoming standard in 1914, six years after the car's introduction. Ford eliminated the other colors after discovering that only black enamel dried fast enough to keep up with his production lines— which increased efficiency and saved money, thus rendering irrelevant every other consideration.

Alfred Sloan's approach to cosmetic issues was more colorful, despite his being the quintessential gray-flannel suit. He did so for marketing reasons, primarily, but also to back-scratch his associates. Beginning in 1917, du Pont family members held a controlling interest in General Motors—and a major product of their namesake chemical company was . . . paint. (By the late 1950s GM was purchasing some $26 million in du Pont products every year.) The du Ponts were forced to sell most of their stake when the Supreme Court ruled, in a 1957 antitrust decision, that the family's GM holdings, and resultant self-dealing, violated the Clayton Act.

Ford's and Sloan's opposing views of car color illustrate their predilections, respectively, for utility and style. But they also underscore the idea of choice—contained, with Ford, in the droll pretense that options exist, and with Sloan, in the accentuation of trivial difference. At bottom both companies offered only a Hobson's choice, that is, no real choice at all; if a customer wanted a car, he had to purchase the sort that car manufacturers, for whatever reasons, had determined to make. Volkswagen, and then Japanese carmakers, in time would exploit this paradox by producing the kind of vehicles that people actually seemed to want, but in the interim automobile buyers were at the mercy of an oligopoly.

An oligopoly, moreover, that produced a cultural monopoly. For how many people in the United States, today, can manage without a car? By the middle 1920s, writes James Flink, the Model T was indispensable to rural life; in the same decade teenagers in southern California already considered the car "a social essential." And our dependence on the automobile has increased exponentially since then; over 200 million motor vehicles are now registered in the United States, more than one for every licensed driver. Another telling factoid: The Department of Transportation says the number of vehicles in this country has grown, over the last thirty years, at *six times* the rate of the human population.

The social consequences of car ownership have been enormous. In the obvious ways—air pollution, traffic jams, road deaths—but in more subtle ways as well. Cars are responsible for the suburb, the mall, the office park, the billboard, even talk radio; for the asphalting of the landscape, the fact that more U.S. land is devoted to autos than to housing. Will that change in the foreseeable future? Probably not. Lewis Mumford once observed that the official U.S. flower should be the cloverleaf, and he's right.

Which brings us to the upside of law school—its ability to highlight important issues. Guido Calabresi, the former dean of Yale Law and now a federal judge, annually submits to his torts class an intellectual riddle called "The Gift of the Evil Deity." The lecture, which focuses on the immense social costs of the automobile, is famous in legal circles: Bill Clinton, I'm told, has quoted from it.

Suppose, Guido asks, that a supernatural power offers the United States something that would make life much more pleasant and convenient. There's only one condition: the grisly death of a thousand people, picked at random, every year. Most students in the tort class reply, without a second thought, that they would reject the offer.

"What's the difference," the dean counters, "between this gift and the automobile?"

The answer, of course, is very little—though the automobile in fact takes more than forty thousand American lives annually, and has snuffed out nearly three million altogether, far more than the sum total of U.S. war deaths. Calabresi's point is clear as day: As a culture we regularly choose convenience over life, however much we publicly deny the trade-off, attempt to hide the choices from ourselves.

We could build much safer cars, but don't, for reasons of cost. We could crack down on drunk and accident-prone drivers, but do so equivocally, because we regard driving almost as a constitutional right. Cars are much safer today than they were thirty years ago, but the improvement can be attributed more to Ralph Nader and his allies than increased driver intelligence or growing guilt among carmakers; the majority of motorists, as Detroit well knows, are willing to gamble with their lives every time they get behind the wheel. It's a baffling fact: We pay thousands of dollars annually to ensure that our medical expenses are paid in the event of a car accident, yet begrudge shelling out for safety features that could render postcrash hospitalization unnecessary.

Our passion for automobiles isn't just a "decision for death," as Calabresi puts it, but a vote for a certain kind of life. Man lost the use of his feet, Emerson wrote in "Self-Reliance," through overreliance on horse-drawn carriages;

with the advent of the automobile he's lost an entire range of freedoms, even as he gains others. Follow, for example, the money. Cars and their support systems absorb more than half a *trillion* dollars annually—in retailing and service and government subsidies—and that's money not spent on public transport, or health care, or education. And think, too, of the countless car-spent hours that isolate us from our communities rather than connecting us to them.

And what it you don't like cars? If you'd rather walk than ride? You're worse off than if the automobile had never been invented, for few Americans today—a few million urbanites aside—can walk to work, to shopping, to school. The automobile is a lock as well as a key, a trap as well as an escape.

I don't know when Les lost interest in cars. His first love was bicycles, but automobiles played a significant role in our relationship from the beginning. As often as not there'd be a half-disassembled car in the driveway, awaiting a replacement part or spare time or simple motivation. Les's Peugeot, in need of an engine rebuild; the tiny Fiat 600, which needed most everything; his parents' 1956 Jaguar XK 140, which Les regularly threatened to fix up. Each car stirs up a raft of memories, even though they spent most of their lives up on blocks.

The Peugeot: It took us camping in the Sierra (with Gar), to the beach for walks with the dogs, gave us a place to sit in Les's burned-out abode (the backseat was portable). The Fiat: I saw it on the road exactly once, a remarkable sight—Les at the wheel with his head sticking out the sunroof, since he was too tall to see through the windshield. The Jag: getting respect, finally, when I helped Les rehabilitate the brake system as a dry run for Seven assembly. (The Jag's grease sleeves were leather, its floorboards partly wood. Which reminds me of the old joke concerning the Brush Runabout, an early, mostly wood car made by the man who designed the first

Cadillac: *wooden body, wooden axles, wooden wheels, would'n' run*.)

I had hoped Les would eventually help me with the Seven, but I realized, as we worked on the Jaguar, that wasn't going to happen. Teaming up for a major project seemed a natural step in our friendship, but I could tell Les had fallen out of love with the mechanical process. He remained a wellspring of technical knowledge—did I know that British airplanes outperformed their German counterparts during World War II because Rolls-Royce engines, being fuel-injected, didn't stall during dives and rolls?—but had suggested the Jag project mostly out of fellowship.

At first I thought Les was simply bored with cars, that familiarity had bred contempt. Over time, though, I concluded that the automobile had come to represent everything Les disliked about modern, material life. He had been shedding possessions for decades, but since moving to Britain in the 1970s his rate of rejection had increased. Strange but true; I think Les had found a soulmate in his aged London landlady . . . and that soul was lodged firmly in the nineteenth century.

Had Mrs. Forsythe ever driven a car, let alone owned one? Doubtful, London being such a walkable city, and easy to traverse by bus or underground. Mrs. Forsythe's needs were minimal, too, for her home was unencumbered by the modern conveniences that seem, after the first appliance darkens the door, to pile on top of one another. Her books were prewar and bound in leather; her furniture, original Victorian; her phone an ancient upright model with a separate earpiece. At one point Mrs. Forsythe had a refrigerator—salvaged and fixed by a tenant, I believe—but if she owned a television or record player, I never saw them.

Between managing the bike shop—where he refused a salary, taking money from the till only when needed—and living with Mrs. Forsythe, Les had removed himself to the far fringes of the Western market system. Here—abetted by Mrs.

Forsythe's other lodgers, usually penny-pinching students at the University of London—he could lead a life free of most twentieth-century vices: money, waste, extravagance, keeping up with the Joneses. Les streamlined his life long before it became fashionable to do so, and one casualty was his fondness for cars.

Thoreau had his cabin, Ford Greenfield Village, Clough Williams-Ellis Portmeirion; Patrick McGoohan had *The Prisoner*, Les his bicycle . . . and I would have my Seven. All were retreats from, and comments upon, the modern world, each of us fleeing in a different way.

Were we driven by fate, upbringing, active choice? The question's unanswerable, but this much I do know: a twist or three in my own DNA and I too would be living on a bicycle, here and then there, going where work, or friends, or urges called.

14

THE WEAKEST LINKS

It's a select crowd, those of us who know the ordinary pocket comb can double as an automotive tool. How select? Probably about the same number as those realizing electrical-box knockout disks are ideal for latching Dzus, the bizarre, originally aeronautic clamps that fasten the Seven's nose cone. For a time I thought about phoning Click and Clack to pass on these helpful hints, but thought better of it.

I discovered the versatility of the pocket comb while wedged, headfirst and essentially upside down, in the Seven's passenger footwell. No, I hadn't fallen in: I was trying to install the handbrake lever. It's a major pain, largely because the aluminum barrel that holds the brake cable, and the sheathing in which the cable slides, are anchored by the same circlip. The problem? You need three hands to keep the components in place, while your fourth—if you happen to have four, like Shiva—searches for the circlip pliers—if you happen to have a pair of those, too. As it turned out, though, a circlip tool would have been useless, for the handbrake assembly doesn't utilize the standard C-shaped clip.

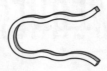

I was about to give up on this particular task, having left my needle-nose pliers on the garage floor, when I felt a jab in my thigh. *Aha! Comb!* Could I save myself a tool backtrack by using a pocket-comb tooth to force the circlip into place? Indeed I could; I held the circlip in position, aligned it with the comb, thumbed the clip from behind, and *pop*, in it went. God—Shiva, perhaps?—does work in mysterious ways.

The handbrake is said to be the only component unchanged from the original Seven, and I believe it. That's not to imply the handbrake is pitifully simple, or unnecessarily complicated; it's quite similar, in truth, to modern handbrakes. The Seven's merely seems antediluvian because it's so awkwardly placed, as if the handbrake were an afterthought—which of course it is, since Seven aficionados are far more interested in going than stopping.

One thing's for sure: No Seven component has received such bad press. Over the years the handbrake's been called "more of an ornament than an effective piece of equipment," "a thing to avoid using," "an unsolved problem," "best forgotten," and something that "must have come from a fire sale." You could regard it as an emergency brake, I guess, and on occasion as a parking brake, but most Seven owners assume the device exists only to comply with safety regulations.

That was my conclusion, certainly, because the handbrake—however functional on paper—seemed unlikely to remain so postinstallation. It's mounted horizontally under the dashboard, for one thing, and only after being bent, rather severely, in a vise. Without the bend the handbrake won't clear the transmission tunnel ... though the manual fails to add that the act of bending may itself (shades of Heisenberg!) cause the mechanism to fail. My handbrake, at least, didn't appreciate rough treatment.

Few people know much about handbrakes, not even the most avid car lover, because they're unsexy and require little attention to boot. The Seven builder gets to know his intimately, however, because the required bend means dismantling it. And I suspect I'm not the only Seven owner who commenced the installation to the sound of a comic-book *sproing*, immediately followed by the *ping* of various metal parts—the pivot bolt, nyloc, pawl, ratchet mechanism, and locking rod—skipping about on the floor. No *pfff*, this time, of bolt hitting tarp, a very familiar sound; John's bench vise was in the basement, so I was, too.

After collecting the wayward hardware—I didn't lose anything, so far as I know (gulp)—I collected myself by performing a less vexing chore: mating the two handbrake cables, which work together like center-pull bicycle brakes. I laid out the front cable, passed the rear cable through the front cable's tensioner, and secured the rear cable's ends to the hooks cast onto each of the rear-brake assemblies. That done, I turned back to the handbrake, still languishing in the vice, and reassembled it properly. I think.

The project took time, for it proved difficult to bend the handbrake housing, and in a separate operation its locking rod, at the same angle. The bends looked identical, but three times I discovered, after performing the upside-down installation stunt, that the handbrake engaged only grudgingly. Eventually I diagnosed the problem; the pawl was getting hung up in the handbrake's housing, which I had overcompressed during the bending procedure. A rod rebend, plus a liberal application of antiseize, fixed things just fine . . . not that I'll bother to use the handbrake, knowing what I know now. As somebody, somewhere, has no doubt said, *If it ain't broke, don't fuck with it.*

Installing the handbrake was frustrating, but a nice break, nonetheless, from routine Seven work—namely, bolting components in place. Days and days overflowing with nut-and-bolt work began to wear thin, until I felt close to a Heathkit Syndrome relapse; assembling by the numbers, learning little, doing no more than sticking Bolt A into Washer B onto Component C with Nut D.

By this time, though, I knew that disdain often masks ignorance. Could there be a theory, an art, behind mechanical connection? Of course, and it even has a bible, *Carroll Smith's Nuts, Bolts, Fasteners and Plumbing Handbook.*

One reason for building the Seven was the desire to travel. Not foreign sojourns, necessarily, nor even local road-tripping, but cultural adventuring—the chance to spend time with people who centered their lives on objects, ideas, totally alien to me. Well, in the Smith book I found an extremely unfamiliar culture—a subculture of one, a car nut who's nuts for car nuts.

Carroll Smith is a race-car engineer, well known for a series of how-to racing books called *Tune to Win, Prepare to Win, Engineer to Win,* and so on. (The book at hand was titled, before national reprinting, *Screw to Win.*) The fastener volume is perhaps the most interesting, because it's a slap in the face to those who take connections for granted. Smith explains why in an opening section disconcertingly titled "Statement of Nonliability" (the author, clearly, expects his words to result in action). A joint, he writes, "is always the weakest link in the structural chain," and the fastener "usually the weakest link in the joint." Nuts and bolts, in other words, are a car's Achilles' heel, and one disregards them at great peril.

I turned to Smith while bringing out, finally, the Seven's heavy artillery—the gearbox and engine. The 'box arrives already bolted to the tailshaft housing, so my job was to connect this assembly to the clutch's bellhousing, and then—hurrah!—the bellhousing to the engine. At that point the now-impressive engine-clutch-gearbox-tailshaft group could be lowered into the engine bay . . . and the Seven would seem, at long last, like a real car.

The assembly, to date, had required mainly standard bolts, but this installation called for metric bolts, too—and more significantly, bolts with "pitches" both coarse and fine. Smith explains the difference: It's a question of whether you want to make the bolt or the bolted more resistant to fatigue; which part, if you're forced to choose, you want to break. Bolts going into metal castings, like engine blocks and gearboxes, carry coarse threads to give the receiving part a larger stress area, and thus make it the stronger element in the connection. A bolt carrying fine threads, by contrast, increases the stress distribution on the bolt itself, making the bolt the stronger element.

I have yet to understand fully, as engineers will no doubt agree, the coarse/fine distinction. But Smith's book did force me to grasp one potentially lifesaving fact—that joints create stress as well as combat it. Stress is bad coming from the wrong direction, since it leads to part-fatigue and fastener-shearing. On the other hand, the proper torquing of a bolt or screw—as the verb, derived from the Latin "to twist," implies—creates positive "tensile" stress, pressure that keeps the fastener in place.

A male thread advances with minimal stress into a female part until the bolt head touches the surface being joined. Tensile stress comes with further turning, when the bolt head has no place to go but its male threads continue to turn against the female threads, thus stretching the bolt and locking it in. It's commonly said that overtightening a bolt is more dangerous than undertightening, but Smith argues, convincingly, the reverse. Undertightened bolts provide less clamping force, and a quality bolt that survives initial tightening has already reached its highest stress point and shouldn't fail in ordinary service.

Such failures do occur, of course, and it's usually the result of poor initial joining—when someone like me hasn't done his torque homework. Examples: the Datsun wheel that threatened to fall off because its lug nuts weren't tightened; the water-pump bolt I overtorqued and broke in the same car; the exhaust system I left on a freeway due to rusted-out retaining bolts. If every car manufacturer used high-quality bolts, and each bolt were properly tightened, scores of lives, hundreds even, might be saved every year.

Smith notes that bolt failures often originate with imperfections on the surface of a bolt, which is why cleaned and polished parts last longer than their scratched and dirty brethren. Now there's a nice little irony: Superficial inspection, sometimes, isn't.

A major draw of the 1939 World's Fair in New York City was General Motors' fantastical "City of Tomorrow." Skyscrapers, suburbs, shopping malls, and business parks, all connected by an elaborate web of seven-plus-lane freeways and ring roads, limited-access interchanges and elevated highways—it was a decidedly utopian vision, and considered unrealistic by many. Today the dream seems dystopian—even though many of the eye-popping innovations introduced at the exhibit were realized within decades. We got what we wanted, in other words . . . and then changed our minds.

It's an old story, the realized dream proving a grievous dis-appointment. But it has special resonance with regard to the automobile, for the car has had such a broad effect on Ameri-can culture, and took so many years to show its dark side. Who could have imagined, when Ford announced his plans to democratize transportation, that so much death and discon-tent would follow? The car, unquestionably, saved and improved millions of lives, but as with nuclear power, its ben-efits were oversold; the drawbacks, once fully accounted for, are substantial. The automobile isn't going to disappear because of its high social costs, as some have argued, but the costs should at least be thoroughly examined.

The root problem is an automotive "tragedy of the com-mons." The phrase was made famous by environmental scien-tist Garrett Hardin, who in 1968 pointed out that every indi-vidual, if given free access to a finite community property, will perforce attempt to maximize his own benefits from it. The result is both inevitable and obvious: The community prop-erty, if unrenewable or unrenewed, will be used up.

And that's what the automobile has done in spades, because cars are voracious eaters. In this country we spend 20 percent of our income on cars; owe more than $400 *billion* in auto loans; use half our energy resources (imported and domestic) to operate road vehicles. And let's not forget that the 1991 Gulf War was fought over the Iraqi threat to U.S. oil supplies, or that Japan attacked Pearl Harbor in response to a U.S. oil embargo. So long as the world's fuel is limited, and man's desires are limitless—we have Alfred Sloan, among others, to thank for that—freedom in the commons will bring, as Hardin put it, "ruin to all."

The oft-predicted "autopia" now seems, to many people, more like "autogeddon."

Hardin's contrast between limited resources and limitless desires, which I came across in an anticar book, put me in mind of "conspicuous consumption." The phrase is often used with regard to cars, especially those from Detroit's salad days; automobile historian John Rae observed that the overblown vehicles of the 1950s "exemplif[ied] Thorstein Veblen's concept of conspicuous consumption on a scale never anticipated by him." I knew the phrase appeared in Veblen's *The Theory of the Leisure Class*, and naturally had to find out whether the author's intended meaning had survived, intact, despite decades of interpretation.

It had, I discovered. But another idea in Veblen's treatise proved more interesting—do you sense a theme here?—than my intended target. (Veblen, incidentally, has also been described, by the social critic Max Lerner, as "the last man who knew everything.")

The higher classes of an industrialized society spurn machine-made goods, Veblen wrote, because such goods are produced efficiently. Why the animus toward efficiency? For the same reason the leisure class appreciates great time wasters like correct spelling and grammar: because wastefulness, of both time and money, is the surest sign of wealth. Besides, machine-made goods can be purchased by most anyone, and there's no point in being rich if you can't buy things beyond others' means.

Rather amusing, this theory, and compelling, too. But then comes Veblen's kicker: While the leisure class disdains manual labor, not to mention the laborer himself, it nonetheless values goods bearing the hallmarks of manual labor. If an item shows the "honorific crudeness" of craftsmanship, or is demonstrably obsolete—can be associated with history and beauty, not sweat and work—the leisure class treasures it, because ownership of the useless item derives purely and obviously from choice, not necessity.

Writers write from a compulsion to understand, a compulsion born from a sense of discomfort with the world. And building the Seven, in John's garage and in my mind, had indeed lessened my unease, my subterranean feelings of ignorance and inadequacy. But this idea of Veblen's cut the other way: Could I really be building the Seven, this vehicle of quintessentially honorific crudeness, to advertise my economic and social freedom? To patronize rather than learn, exploit rather than experience? I hoped not, but those questions remain unanswered to this day.

There was solace, though, in the predictability of my arrival at this self-questioning point. The search for answers, for an understanding of will and destiny and conviction, for the identity of Number One, inevitably brings you back to yourself . . . for what else is there to believe, to believe in? I, for one, am capable of doubting everything, and until self-doubts are resolved, no other view can escape suspicion. When you round up the usual suspects, in my world, you round up everyone.

15

TWIST AND SHOUT

Tailshaft, transmission, custom adapter, clutch bellhousing, engine—the array in the driveway looks like a 1950s sci-fi ray gun. With all the bells and whistles, too: Caterham ships the engine with a slew of accessory parts installed, including the distributor, the fuel pump, and the dual Weber carburetors. The latter makes the engine look so top-heavy I wondered, for a time, whether the whole thing was going to tip over.

The battery was already mounted in the chassis, so I didn't have to worry about getting it in before the engine—in some Sevens, because of interfering frame members, you can't change the battery without first removing a carburetor. Not the greatest design, I thought—but felt better after looking at the manual and realizing what other builders went through. If I'd decided on the four-speed Escort Sport transmission, for example, I'd be grinding down part of the gearbox, opening it up, and replacing the reverse-gear stop; if I'd opted for the Vauxhall engine, I'd be installing what the manual called "a crunch washer (dowty seal)." None of my reference books, not even my auto dictionary, defined "dowty."

The power assembly was quite impressive, all in all, and I sincerely doubted it would fit inside the engine bay. Did Sears carry giant shoehorns?

What I needed, of course, was the shoehorn's big brother, an engine hoist. Most rental centers carry them, fortunately, so I asked John if he'd help me transport one with his Datsun work truck. He agreed, we set off a few mornings later, and by ten-thirty the hoist was up and stabilized on home asphalt.

I centered a length of heavy-duty chain on the hoist's hook and bolted its terminal links to opposite ends of the engine block. John pumped the hoist jack and slowly, slowly, up the assembly went. The engine looked ungainly twisting in the air—and to think that such things launched hundreds of millions of cars from zero to sixty in a few seconds every day, it fairly boggled the mind.

We admired the engine for a while, reluctant to start. The assembly was delicate in places: The pin that turns the speedometer cable, for example, stuck out entirely unprotected. The pin also clicks the odometer over, which seems a natural secondary function—unlike, say, running the windshield wipers, which the speedo cables on 1940s Citroën 2CVs also did. Early versions of that model, the French equivalent of the VW Beetle, had a top speed of about 35 mph, so the wipers often flapped with excruciating slowness.

If I left off the speedometer cable—and some Seven racers probably do—I could have driven the Seven for years without registering a single mile. That's illegal, of course, and means disabling the speedometer as well, but the alteration isn't as difficult as you might think. I had learned as much a few years earlier, in a rental car whose speedometer stubbornly registered 0 even as I raced taxicabs through yellow lights. I considered returning the car, but in those dark days rental companies still charged by the mile. The agent just grunted (this was New York City) when, days later, I returned the car and mentioned the problem; then he added a single mile to the odometer reading, presumably so the company's central computer wouldn't freak out.

More parts went on. I screwed the backup light switch into the transmission housing; an electrical circuit was completed, I guessed, when you notched the gear shift into reverse. (I didn't buy a used Toyota once because a similar switch, for the brake lights, was dreadfully positioned—under the brake pedal, so you heard an annoying click whenever you pulled up to a stop sign.) I bolted mounting blocks onto the chassis, a matched pair to support the engine, another the gearbox. I considered putting in the hydraulic clutch cylinder, but couldn't find it once again, which was just as well. Like the speedo drive pin, the cylinder was vulnerable during engine installation.

John and I would have hemmed and hawed for days were it not for the ticking of the hoist's rental clock. There was nothing to do but proceed, which we did with jangling nerves.

I can't speak for John, but I felt like Prince Charming holding the glass slipper. *Cinderella sure is beautiful, this looks a good, tight fit, and yet . . .*

John pumped the jack again, brought the carburetors to chest height, and nudged the hoist forward until the engine hovered over the car. I pushed down lightly on the tailshaft, then maneuvered it into the Seven's empty bowels as John gradually lowered the engine.

An inch to the right; the throttle might bump the cross-bar—

yes, that one. Too far; the starter-motor housing's going to bash the curtain rod, I mean the steering column.

Wait.

Didn't the manual say something about removing the steering column on De Dion cars before ... before *what?* Back to section 9.4.3: Oh, good, that must be right-hand-drive cars.

Never mind.

Okay, John, more, yes, right, no no no not "right," I mean "correct."

Down, in; down, in; down, in: We bootlegged the assembly into position, until I could crawl under the Seven and witness the tailshaft's progress toward the propshaft. By now the gap was only a couple inches—so narrow, in fact, I could grab the tailshaft, pull, and make the components kiss.

John lowered the engine incrementally and the shaft began, ever so slowly, to penetrate the housing. "Down" movement almost magically became "in," the engine having nowhere else to go. Minutes earlier I had berated myself for failing to rent, as the manual recommended, a trolley jack with which to support and manipulate the transmission, but the tool proved unnecessary. When I twisted the propshaft for the fourth time, the engine assembly shrugged onto it, the prop's splines suddenly deciding to shiver up to their mates in the gearbox.

John lowered the hoist arm still more, the engine shrugged again, and settled squarely onto the chassis mounts.

"That's it," I cried from under the car, inchworming out to retrieve the engine-mount bolts. I started, hastily, to screw them in.

"That's it? Really?"

John looked surprised, even disappointed, for the much anticipated installation had been brisk and uneventful. But it was a build highlight nonetheless: When people asked to look under the car's bonnet, there was, finally, something to show.

Within a few hours I emptied an entire shelf of parts. On went the starter motor, into its bellhousing hollow; the ignition coil and its bracket, by way of bolts to the firewall. (Bolts rather than rivets because the coil, too, must be removed to replace the Seven's battery.) The oil-pressure switch screwed into the cylinder block, the water-temperature sender into the cylinder head.

I connected the wires to the radiator fan, and the red cable linking the positive battery terminal to the starter. "DO NOT CONNECT THE EARTH AT THIS STAGE," the manual barked, so I didn't. No doubt it's happened—a Seven going up in flames, days from completion, a careless electrical ground rendering the ashen builder carless.

I foresaw myself acquiring new skills while building the Seven, but among them was not the oral siphoning of transmission fluid. As with the differential, I failed to add lubricant before installing the component—only this time I exacerbated the problem, because when I did fill the gearbox, I overfilled it. Adding fluid to the diff was hard, so naturally the job I *didn't* have to do, draining it, was easy (because the drain plug's accessible, on the bottom of the diff); filling the transmission was easy—you unbolted the cover—so draining it, just as naturally, was impossible—the transmission's side-mount plug was blocked by the driveshaft tunnel. I had made the inverse—the contrapositive?—of my earlier lubricant mistake.

I called Chris. *It's okay to overfill the transmission a little, right?*

Wrong.

"You've got to bring it down," he said, "till you can feel the fluid when you stick your finger in the plughole." Too high a level, he continued, would cause needless drag on the gears, which not only wasted energy but stressed the transmission and could cause premature breakdown.

The excess fluid would have to go. And since the drain plug was inoperative, and the tightly packed transmission gears left no room for ladling, my only recourse was the siphon.

This was frustrating news, for installation of the engine had set me free for different, less stressful work. Attaching the front fenders, which gave the car a racy splash of red; preparing the air horns and compressor, which awaited only drill holes; determining the exact position of the heater and the radiator-overflow bottle. The last thing I wanted to do was something boring and familiar . . . though purging the excess transmission fluid was, as it turned out, neither. When my vacuum-bulb siphon failed, I had to perform the task—yuck—by mouth.

The siphon, truth be told, didn't give out so much as become irksome. I was pumping away, moving fluid into a bottle at a sluggish rate, when it dawned on me that the apparatus really was a siphon—that gravity could do the work. All I had to do was suck the air out of the tube, put it in the fluid, and make sure the exit point was lower than the transmission. A nice solution, I thought—but a failure, because the tube was too narrow and the fluid too thick to flow (gee, didn't I run into this bottleneck before?). I wiped off the siphon tube and set in motion a more primitive system. *Three quick pulls, breathe, three quick pulls, breathe; transfer the tube, now full, to the bottle, and blow out the fluid.*

I got an impressive aerobic workout. *Suck, breathe, expel, rest,* and *feel the burn* . . . of transmission fluid, when I sucked too hard. Dizzy Gillespie, had he been in the neighborhood, would have wanted a hoseful.

The fluid, ten minutes later, had returned to the proper level. I was happy to discover that in some situations, at least, my body was its own best tool—and happier that no one (so far as I know) had witnessed my using it.

I replaced the transmission cover, bolted the washer-bottle clamp above it, ran the speedo cable from the drive pin to the dashboard, test-fit the windshield and its seemingly toy wipers. I installed the gas tank's filler hose and the boot's wooden floor, clamped on the fuel cap, poured a gallon of 104-octane gasoline in the Seven's tiny tank. *Man, was I getting close!*

I connected the carburetors to the gas pedal with the throttle cable, bolted the gearshift into the gearbox, screwed on the shift knob. Could I resist climbing into the still-seatless Seven and running through the gears while stabbing the accelerator? Of course not.

If you hang out with British car nuts you will see, sooner or later, the T-shirts and bumper stickers referring to Joseph Lucas as the "Prince of Darkness." It's a joke, of course: The electrical products of Lucas Ltd., like so many English car parts, are not the most reliable. At some point you'll also hear this gag: Why do the English drink their beer warm? Because they have Lucas refrigerators. Not to mention the innumerable Lotus jokes, many quite good. What does Lotus stand for? Lots Of Trouble, Usually Serious.

Automotive electrical systems, as most every driver knows, can be immensely frustrating. Even the best manufacturers suffer from electrical glitches: Toyota was humbled a decade ago when at least a score of Camry owners discovered, after an electric relay stuck open and melted the door-controlling solenoids, that they were locked in. Most drivers, luckily, escaped without too much trouble—they crawled out the trunk, having remembered that the car's backseat folds down.

Britain, along with Italy, produces Europe's most notorious electrics. That makes (perverse) sense; a bad-weather country renowned for good-weather cars might as well go whole hog and take an irrational approach to its cars' most weather-vulnerable feature. Rain isn't the only thing, either, that makes British electrics fail. Emerson Fittipaldi tells of returning to his personal Lotus Elan, after winning yet another Grand Prix race for Colin Chapman, and being forced to bump-start the car due to a chronic electrical drain.

Kit-car builders are stymied more often by electrics than anything else. The numerous circuits that make up the wiring loom—the car's electrical backbone—go every which way, are easily confused, often fragile, and invariably idiosyncratic; it's a rare car that's free, on completion, from an electrical bug or two. The Seven builder is luckier than most, though, for its loom is installed at the factory. My main electrical job, consequently, should have been no more complicated than connecting various switches and lights and relays to the appropriate loom wires.

The process, surprisingly, is almost as simple as it sounds. You do, of course, encounter eccentricities—eleccentricities?—but they tend to be amusing rather than frustrating. The Seven, for example, uses wood in its electrical system— yet another similarity with the Morgan, which boasts a wooden frame. So what if the Seven's timber isn't English ash but blocks of scrap wood, used to moor the taillights to the fenders?

There's a comparable inelegance to the horn switch. Its migration from dashboard to steering hub was delayed for decades, I suspect, on electrical grounds (pun unintended but likely accurate), for today's horn is activated in a byzantine manner. A tiny metal bar, damped with a spring, sticks out the backside of the hub and constantly scribes a copper ring encircling the steering-column tube. When you lean on the horn, an electrical connection is made inside the hub, resulting in—if you've added the recommended air bugles—the Seven's raise-the-dead PAAAAARP. This is progress?

Caterham had already installed most of the Seven's dashboard gauges and switches, so making them operational was a matter of connecting the proper leads. I stuck the key in the ignition, turned it to the battery position, and voilà—the fan spun, the wipers slapped, the fuel gauge rose. The brake-test light didn't work, and neither did the emergency flashers, though I expected the latter since I had yet to hook up the turn signals. By the next day they too were operative, again without muss or fuss.

Getting the electrical system to work wasn't nearly as problematic as I had anticipated. Its swift completion did, however, create a problem of its own: fear, a substantial and immediate by-product of the Seven's being nearly roadworthy. Once I tightened the suspension, installed the seats, and anchored the exhaust system, the car would be ready for a test drive.

The exhaust went on, initially, without a hitch. Apply high-temp silicone seal between the upper exhaust manifold and the engine, then bolt away; spread muffler compound between the upper and lower manifolds, between the muffler and the tailpipe, then twist to make a good bond. You twisted for other reasons as well—because the exhaust system was full of bends, and thus difficult, at times, to line up. The bends inside the engine bay were fairly easy to deal with, as was the bend taking the system to the muffler—positioned outside the car, next to the driver's seat, and probably the most common source of Seven injury (burned legs).

I had trouble only with the postmuffler bend, for a few inches beyond the exhaust it took a ninety-degree left, back under the chassis, and then an immediate ninety-degree right, before it straightened out to meet the tailpipe. If the exhaust wasn't twisted just so and secured instantly in place, this S-shaped section was sure to rub on the Scylla of the left-rear tire or the Charybdis of the bolt securing the A-frame. I tried one rotation after another before arriving, two hours later, at an acceptable alignment, and wasn't happy even then. The exhaust missed the tire by less than an inch, a suspension member by half an inch, and emerged maybe three-eighths of an inch beneath the Seven's fiberglass tail. *Will the clearance disappear when the car settles on the bushings? During hard cornering? The hot emissions—could they melt the 'glass?*

Chris didn't seem too concerned when I told him my worries. He did, however, make a suggestion: If I saw any signs of interference, now or in the future, flatten the S bend with a ball-peen hammer until the interference disappeared. This bit of advice was not exactly inspiring, and I didn't follow it in the end; I refit the exhaust instead, and this attempt, for reasons unknown, produced greater clearance almost everywhere.

Now came the litmus test.

A new engine isn't fragile, exactly, but still needs careful treatment. My block, enlarged from Ford's standard-issue 1,600cc and modified with a racing cylinder head, had no doubt been lubricated for a factory test run, but I wasn't taking any chances. (The Vauxhall engine's bellhousing has been known to arrive with sand still in it, stubborn remains of the aluminum casting process.) I called both Chris and Les for advice. Chris was away, racing at an Atlanta speedway, but Les suggested I add oil to the block, as after a rebuild, to prevent piston binding and scraping.

I did so, dripping oil through the spark-plug openings. But I chickened out with the ignition key in my hand: I decided to delay starting the engine until the seats and carpeting were in. It was a strange equipoise, my optimistic side champing at the bit to crank things up while my pessimistic side, fearing massive failure, hoped to defer the main event as long as possible.

It's for good reason the final trimming of a car is called "detailing." The various carpets turned me into a seamstress, cutting darts, affixing snaps, cropping here and tacking there to get just the right fit. The rug work took a couple of days, as did the seats. The latter operation was eyebrow raising, though, for each seat was attached to the frame only by four standard-issue bolts. Rammed in just the right place by another car, it seemed, and they'd be transformed into James Bond ejector seats.

Start day arrived fourteen months after I collected the Seven kit in Cambridge. The weather had warmed enough to warrant pushing the car outside—a good thing, for I anticipated clouds of gasoline fumes, burned and otherwise.

I made a second cup of coffee in Jenny's kitchen to energize myself, or maybe put off the moment of truth. If the engine refused to kick over I'd suspect a bad electrical connection ... but really, who knew? The carbs could be misadjusted, the fuel line clogged, the distributor damaged, the throttle cable poorly tensioned, the starter gear unmeshed. *We'll drive off that bridge when we come to it. . . .*

Gas pedal pulls carb throttle in a smooth arc, returns when released? *Check.* Battery cables firmly attached, battery properly grounded? *Check.* Radiator fan rotates correctly, belt and thermostat in place? *Check.* No cooling- or fuel-system leaks? *Check.* Plenty of radiator fluid, plenty of fuel? *Check.* Enough oil, as per dipstick? *Check.* Transmission in neutral, handbrake (for what it's worth) engaged? *Check.* Nerves impossibly jittery? *No question.*

My heart was in my mouth as I eased into the driver's seat. It did fit like a glove, as others have observed. I ran through the gears again, hoping to increase my confidence; squirmed as long as humanly possible; and after saying a silent prayer, turned the ignition key.

One click: The high-beam reminder light went on, as did the lights themselves. I thumbed the toggle and—*phew*—the headlights turned off. Two clicks: Another idiot light went on, for battery engagement. *Good—I mean* Oops, *forgot to prime the engine.*

Four pumps on the pedal, six, eight, ten should be plenty, right? *Fumes, smell 'em, that's good, I think, the gas is getting there.* One more twist of the key, three clicks, and . . . nothing.

Shit.

Try again. Nothing.

More gas? *A long way to go, after all, and the fuel lines were dead empty.*

Four more pumps, again nothing.

Goddam, I've probably flooded the engine now, have to wait and start all over. Shit and shinola.

A minute later: *I can't wait any longer, I can't.*

Once more into the breach . . .

The engine shudders.

Jesus Christ, it tried to turn over!

Adrenaline rush.

More gas?

Twist the key, again nothing; twist once more, the engine repeats its shudder, but longer this time and dieseling before dying.

Shit yes, this thing's gonna start!

Turn key, engine groan, stomp the accelerator and the motor roars, *by God it's going to catch,* fumes distorting the air around the carburetors, mash the pedal again and the engine races high, then dies.

Think, think; think.

Yes, it'll work. *Just first-start balky, air in the fuel system maybe, the added cylinder oil.* If it doesn't catch this time, check the plugs for fouling. *Keep the fuel flowing, revs up, get the engine warm, to idle, maybe 1,200, 1,400 revs.*

Man, if I can idle I can drive the damn thing, reverse it into the garage! If I've got reverse . . .

Ignition on, *Christ almighty, idiot lights are pulsing*—the battery's already running down. Does John have a charger? *Now, now, a couple more chances or wait for another day. This time, please.*

Pivot key, battery light on, engine straining . . . but it does catch, *bang bang bang* I'm banging on the accelerator, pedal literally to the metal no carpet there, engine crescendos when I pump, 3,200 rpm tops, threatens to stall when I stop, car itself isn't shaking much, good, likewise engine, good, no nasty rattles (that I can hear), not too much smoke, fumes not so bad now.

The dare: Ease off the gas, engine falls back to 2,000 revs, *okay, too far, oops,* tap again, *yeah,* running rough of course, *easy to fix,* a great sound altogether, really, tap again, I'm grinning like a fool, *sure,* some exhaust pop, a little scary but not much, look down at the gauges and back at the exhaust, *yeah looks good, but who am I to judge. . . .*

Okay finally *this is it*—foot off the accelerator. Down to 1,800 rpm, 1,500, will it hold, *yes . . .*

But why's it racing up, uh-oh, 1,400 then 1,800 by itself, *grease the cable maybe,* okay I'll tweak the accelerator, to 2,200, *right,* down to 1,400, sounds good, *what the hell's the proper idle,* wait and see, wait and see. . . .

Amazing, it's steady, 1,400–1,500, minor stumbling, *yes yes yes* it holds!

The fucker runs, it works! Yes!—oh *shit,* check the radiator temp, *okay,* just out of the blue, *we're okay.*

I scrambled out of the car triumphant, engine running, arms akimbo, Peter Pan after vanquishing Captain Hook. *Don't wanna grow up, not me not I not me.*

I walked around the Seven, checking for oversights, but found none. My senses were indescribably alive: I drank in the noise, the smell, the vibration, the success. This was the end of the line, the beginning of the road; put on the bonnet—*what the hell, don't*—and I could drive around the block. The damn car was *real*!

A *whir* spun my head around. *Shit!* Not an air-leak hiss, not a hose-break splutter—what? *Stop the engine!* No—I know what that is, from VWs in parking lots—the radiator fan kicking in, right? Sure enough, there it is, spinning, automatically engaged by the thermostat—*it works, too!*

Thermostat? *Right, check it,* getting toward red, idling too high probably, too much high revving. *Buddy, now I shut you down.*

I dropped into the car, killed the engine, and fell back in the seat with a mixture of relief and ecstasy. *How many people have done* this?

I clambered out and pushed the Seven into the garage, still grinning, not thinking to reverse it in. No matter; this cake didn't need icing.

But it got some anyway. At lunchtime the next day, after setting the engine idle and tuning the carburetors, I called Lisa. She said I'd better hurry home; I did, we took a cab to the hospital, and early that evening we were parents once more.

Matthew, three at this writing, likes trains.

16

ON THE ROAD

I took the Seven for a spin the following week. Once warm the engine ran evenly, and loudly, and it felt right. The brakes were foremost in my mind, however, as John's neighborhood is hilly and full of blind, twisting turns. The brakes worked fine in the driveway, favoring no wheel and resistant at the pedal, but I knew things could be different on the street.

To turn left or right, that was the question—the road sloped either way. I elected to go uphill, putting my faith in the engine rather than the brakes . . . and ignoring the fact that if both failed I'd be hurtling downhill, backward, and out of control. Ah, for a normal, effective, factory-installed handbrake!

I gunned the engine pulling into the street, and the car

sped briskly up the incline, spinning the tach like an altimeter. The Seven wanted out of first gear in no time, and I obliged after testing the brakes. We (I have to say "we") were going thirty-five in a matter of seconds, well above the first-run top speed I had intended—and it felt like fifty, with the wind whistling, the car jouncing on frost-heaved pavement, the engine wailing as if it yearned for a straightaway. The transmission shifted flawlessly, the braking was predictable, and the engine accelerated without hesitation and slowed with only minor protests.

I waited for something to go wrong—would the brakes blow first, or the radiator, or the clutch?—but anxiety was soon displaced by a sense of conquest. The car stopped at stop signs, surged on acceleration, coiled through curves with enthusiasm, growled up precipitous grades as if they were desert flats. All this during one lap around the block!

I returned to John's house before something did indeed go wrong. What was left? I'd have to go through the assembly manual again, make a list of unfinished items, and check them off one by one. The car seemed fine, now . . . but soon I'd be driving it to Brookfield, where Lisa and I had bought an old farmhouse. We had been forced to move, pretty much: I needed a garage for the Seven.

That's what I told friends, at least. The real reason was Matthew's imminent arrival, and New York's being no place to raise children. Our city friends noted we could see a slice of Riverside Park from our apartment bedroom, but I thought of Codornices, the park in Berkeley in which I spent many youthful hours. Lisa and Thea and I spent a month in Berkeley two years earlier, and the contrast was stark: In Codornices most children were looked after by a parent, and you didn't fear the late-afternoon arrival of older kids, of aggressive panhandlers, of sunset. Only in Riverside Park was I accosted by unfamiliar children demanding I buy them ice cream.

Lisa was apprehensive about the move, having spent most of her life within a single Manhattan zip code. But her ties were loosening, too, for she'd elected not to return to book editing after her maternity leave ran out. It wasn't a difficult choice; Lisa's publishing house, recently taken over by a media conglomerate, declined to acquire a number of literary manuscripts she brought to the editorial board in the months before Thea's arrival. (Foolishly, it turned out, for one of those titles would become, for another publisher, a gigantic best-seller.) The writing was on the wall: Money had gone center stage even in literary culture, providing one more reason to leave town.

It took a few days, over a span of six weeks, to make the Seven roadworthy. I spent much of that time in confidence-building excursions. Jenny was my first passenger: She betrayed fear only during corners, holding on to the side of the car for dear life. I astonished schoolchildren: They rubber-necked while walking home from the bus stop, often waving or shouting "cool!" I annoyed at least one adult: A senior-citizen gardener put hands to hips as I zoomed by.

I could imagine her cognitive dissonance—turning that first spade of sun-warmed soil, glad to have winter done with, only to be assaulted by carburetors at full throat. But did she have to call the cops? It was close: Ten minutes later, sixty seconds after the Seven was safely hidden behind the garage door, the streets were crawling with police cars. I have no doubt they were responding to the gardener's complaint about a too-fast, too-noisy, too-dangerous-looking convertible.

By early June the Seven was ready, from my perspective, to hit the road. The Authorities, of course, thought otherwise; without a registration card, an emissions sticker, a safety check, or license plate, the Seven was supposed to be trailered everywhere. Trailering would have cost hundreds of dollars, though, because I'd have to rent a truck with a hitch as well as a trailer; my Subaru couldn't haul a go-cart, let alone another auto. I decided to take my chances. The Seven was by nature an irresponsible car, and if its designer happily thumbed his nose at the law, well, maybe I should, too.

I decided to drive to Brookfield on a weekday evening, when the cops might be less watchful. John and I debated whether I'd be better off borrowing a license plate or driving plate-naked, and it seemed a toss-up; without a plate the Seven would be a running infraction—but I'd be in real trouble if caught with the wrong plate. Then again, we'd be in New York State for most of the trip, and the cops might not bother with the Seven if it appeared to be registered in Connecticut. On the other hand, from their point of view, a roadster was born trouble, a challenge, could be . . .

Might as well be hanged for a sheep as for a lamb. I unscrewed the Subaru's front plate and put it on the Seven's rear, cheering myself with the notion that a night in jail could make good copy.

Drive Day arrived. After dinner, fully tanked on high-octane coffee, I announced it was time to bite the bullet. I was jazzed, and John, no doubt picking up on my manic behavior, suggested he and Jenny join the procession—Lisa was already planning to follow me in our other clapped-out wagon, an '85 Colt Vista (a direct hand-me-down from brother David) already packed with flotsam and jetsam needing to get to Connecticut. I reluctantly agreed, saying the Seven was probably the most reliable vehicle of the lot—and that I'd never forgive John if the Rabbit ended up on the wrong end of his tow rope.

It was nearly ten by the time we stepped onto John's driveway. The evening was cool, and I had to borrow a windbreaker to avoid getting chilled—I was already shivering and sweating, and not from the weather. I started the Seven, chattered nervously with John as it warmed up, and then turned on the headlights.

I had so many worries it's difficult to single one out as particularly troubling, but I was greatly relieved when the Seven's lights came on and stayed that way. They seemed the night's weakest link; I couldn't help imagining a headlight-killing electrical short-out at fifty miles per hour. I once drove two hundred night miles in a car with inoperative headlights—I tailgated a friend making the same trip—and didn't care to repeat the experience . . . even if the moon, this time, *was* nearly full.

Driving the Seven at night was an eerie affair. You experienced the standard sensory overload of any Seven outing, but it was far stranger in the dark, because the information you absorbed was lower in quantity yet deeper in quality. Engine clamor dominated, of course, but you also noticed the noise-shadows produced by trees, the changes in atmospheric pressure and density. Your night senses seemed dramatically sharper in the Seven, to the point that the car almost seemed to disappear.

That's what I felt, at least, as I drove the village streets leading to the Saw Mill Parkway. Thereafter the story was different, for the road was being rebuilt. At the best of times the Saw Mill is narrow, hilly, full of unanticipated turns and sudden stoplights; under construction it was a wreck, old pavement torn away, lanes narrowed by cement and orange-plastic barriers, shoulders obliterated by construction equipment. All this I had forgotten when planning my northeast passage, insulated by the creature comforts of my still well-sprung, air-conditioned, radio-equipped Subaru. Only when I pulled onto the parkway did I remember what lay ahead.

I drove in the slow lane, John and Lisa in procession behind. Gradually, imperceptibly, I began to relax . . . until new headlights appeared in the rearview mirror, when I squeezed the steering wheel in a death grip.

Is the driver paying attention? Drunk? Is he going to see me, crowd me; carrying yahoos, just waiting to slam-dunk beer cans into roadsters? I'd never driven the Seven on a four-lane road: *What's a minivan going to seem like alongside, or a big old Lincoln—Christ, a tractor-trailer, when we hit the interstate!—if parked Hondas tower over me?*

A Mercedes zoomed by in a heartbeat, going ninety, a hundred. Or so I thought, until five more cars passed me at the same clip. We had driven five miles by then, but I had yet to look at the speedometer: I was too fearful—*let the deer be smart tonight, please*—to take my eyes off the road. Finally, though, I dared.

Jesus! I was doing seventy! Wait: Seventy? *The speed limit's fifty! No, look again—which numbers are kilometers? The yellow ones:* right. *I was really doing . . .* forty-five!

Sure felt like seventy. I sped up reluctantly, to avoid being an obstacle. The adjustment was prudent, but mistimed; two minutes later we reached the first construction zone. A wild and frightening ride: The asphalt was gone, and the Seven jackhammered up and down on the rocky underlayment, *tick-tick-tick*ing and *bam-bam-bam*ming on every hump and hollow. I held on for dear life . . . and barely hard enough, for when we hit the old pavement on an unrefurbished bridge, the steering wheel was nearly torn out of my hands.

The Seven ricocheted away, bent on crashing into the temporary lane dividers, but a panic attack (mine) brought the car back under control. The same incident in the Subaru would have been uneventful, which meant the Seven's wheels were probably misaligned. Nothing I could do about that right then, at least: I had to press on.

I was better prepared for subsequent construction areas, and by the time we reached Pleasantville the worst of the drive was over. Thirty minutes later we merged onto I-684, but wary of patrolmen, soon exited onto a parallel two-lane highway. On this stretch, perhaps twenty miles from our new home, I began to understand what fun the Seven could be. Thick forests, a deserted road, the moon shining on country lakes, through glowing, unhurried clouds; even in darkness the car forced you to drink in the immediate. The highway curved upward, and I took its turns at higher and higher speeds, barreling up banked inclines to feel gratifying g-forces, to bask in the engine's enthusiastic response.

On the far side of one hill we encountered a treeless bottomland, the air dense and misty damp. Instantly I noticed the smells—thick boggy wetness, first, then a trace, just a whiff, of skunk. After that a rich and peaty aroma, then wild onion, and other scents I couldn't place. We were driving through an identifiable ecosystem, and it seemed to be flowing right into the car, waiting to be appreciated, assimilated; a simple, incongruous, unexpected gift. I've never experienced the like, not during thousands of bicycle miles, hundreds of camping miles, and never, certainly, in another automobile. Yes: *This is what the Seven's about.*

Nothing could wipe the smile from my face as I pulled into the driveway, shooting gravel left and right (*must get it paved—a business expense?*). I was in such good spirits, indeed, that a couple miles earlier I had tooted the horn while passing Brookfield's police headquarters. *Let 'em catch me, if they can. As for Number Two, well I'll outrun Rover, too. . . .*

I almost jumped out of my skin when Les showed up. I knew he was coming, but Les operates on Indian time (as it used to be called); he hoped to arrive one particular July week, the day depending on the heat, the roads, the traffic, the weather, the adventures, the will, the ailments (mechanical and personal). Les guessed that cycling to Brookfield from Santa Barbara, where he was attending to family matters, would take six weeks, but I had only the vaguest notion of when he would roll in.

I was sweeping out the barn, the Seven's new home, when someone began talking as if at the office watercooler. Adrenaline shot into every one of my capillaries, my viscera practically exploded in fright; standing in silhouette before me was a large Vietnamese man taking rice to market on his bike. Les, of course, equipped for the road: homemade shirt and patched, hand-sewn trousers; beat-up, found-by-the-highway sunglasses; a construction hard hat turned sun shade with a wide, scrap-cloth brim. The "rice" was Les's worldly goods, collected in various ratty bike bags.

The effect was terrifying, for the getup made Les seem an outerplanetary refugee. I wasn't surprised to learn that some people had nixed Les's request to camp overnight on their property, that others had attempted to slip him money (he refused it).

I hadn't seen Les in two years. He was much the same; new tan lines and major muscles, but Les still resembled . . . well, a vagrant. And the bike, of course, was as jerry-rigged as Les's cycling outfit; mud guards patched with wired-on scraps of plastic, handlebars swollen with cushioning foam and yards of colored tape, pink toe-clips rescued from some trash pile, a seat worn down and weathered to a glossy finish. One look and you'd assume, rightly, that the rider owned nothing worth stealing, including the bike itself.

I had invited Les to Connecticut to help me put up a hundred-foot run of picket fence, but I figured he couldn't resist working on the Seven. A couple of tasks remained: aligning the front wheels, which the trip from Hastings had pushed to the top of the to-do list; rehabilitating the emergency flashers and the brake-warning light, which had never worked. Les knew about such things, but more importantly, would be good company during the troubleshooting process. Chris had already told me how to perform the alignment with string and chalk, and that the electric glitches almost certainly resulted from bad connections, so I was ready to go.

It took a while, though, before I fell in synch with Les, workwise. He hadn't had a regular paycheck, or schedule, in decades; over the years he'd taken a profusion of jobs for ready cash, but usually worked either to fill gaps in his knowledge or for simple companionship. I, on the other hand, had deadlines to meet, a career to advance, plus a growing family and bills to pay; it was difficult, now, to separate work from wages, to give every task its due—to approach a job, in short, as a pleasure instead of a chore. Working with Les was like entering a time machine set to an agrarian age: His day was calibrated by the sun and mealtimes, with many hours set aside for idle conversation, contemplation of the project at hand, and equipment care.

We eventually got around to the wheel alignment, though our improvements, I later discovered, were minimal. The electrical problems occupied a couple afternoons, but here Les and I made real progress; by temporarily bridging fuses we tracked down the flasher's delinquency to a faulty solder joint. We never determined the brake-warning light's problem, but that failure was alleviated by our success with the flasher—particularly since the soldering mistake wasn't mine. It wasn't the last time that a flaw for which I initially took the blame belonged, in fact, on Caterham's doorstep.

Two weeks later, with the Seven fully functional, we went for a spin on a steep, hairpin-filled road leading to a nearby lake. I was roaring through a curve near the top of the ridge, the engine purring away nicely, when Les asked suspiciously, "Is it raining?" He pointed to the windshield, on which a smattering of small, translucent drops had suddenly appeared. I assumed they were late-fallen dewdrops or nectar or tree sap, but glanced at the instrument panel anyway—and saw the oil pressure heading rapidly toward zero.

Fifteen seconds later we reached the lake, pulled over, and removed the bonnet. Oil was dripping from most every engine-bay component; the incoming oil-cooler hose had torn open at its brass fitting.

After visiting the Caterham works two years earlier I was convinced that oil coolers could do more harm than good. I told Chris as much, but he persuaded me to install the option anyway: British driving conditions were quite different, Chris said, adding that I'd be extremely glad to have the cooler during my next New England–summer traffic jam. No doubt he's right—although I thought differently while staring at the cooler's gaping hose, miles from home with an undriveable Seven.

The breakdown proved minor in the end, even providential. The rupture lent itself to a quick fix; we'd simply bypass the oil cooler, taking the good, outgoing hose from the cooler's pump and detouring it right back into the oil system. For that salvage operation, however, we needed a wrench, and I had neglected—stupidly, and unlike any minimally rational British car owner—to put a tool kit in the boot. We had rolled to a stop a hundred yards from a marina, however, and the owner was still working on a boat. At six in the evening he lent us a wrench and two quarts of oil, we made the hose swap, and got back to the house before dinner.

With the Seven once more in good running order, all the car required was inspection by Chris and legalization by the state. The latter was the obvious next step, since Wethersfield, headquarters of Connecticut's motor vehicle department, was much closer than Cambridge.

The Wethersfield trip would be a longer, more rural version of the Hastings–Brookfield expedition, but for some reason I was more apprehensive about police activity. I decided to leave Brookfield by four in the morning, intending to arrive at the DMV hours before it opened at eight.

The Seven was indeed cacophonous with the top up, as I'd been forewarned. But I had no choice; the night was drizzly and cool, not to mention dark, so I was destined to endure for hours the dull grinding of the differential, the booming echoes of the enclosed cockpit, the fogged-up windshield. This last annoyance I solved, before too long, with the fan and defroster—*more parts that worked!*—but the net effect was a car normally conducive to the appreciation of nature becoming an industrial-strength noisemaker.

I had expected to spend two hours in the Seven that night, but the drive took nearly three. I made some wrong turns, true, but the delay was largely a result of country roads bisecting innumerable small towns, each with a stoplight or two. For the first hour I didn't see another moving car; by five, though, the state was beginning to wake up, with most vehicles seemingly headed toward the nearest donut shop (the one business invariably well lit, I learned, before dawn). The traffic got heavier as I approached the DMV, its parking lot already well populated when I pulled in at six-thirty.

Sleeping in the Seven was surprisingly easy, and more comfortable than driving with the top up. By putting a sweater behind my head and folding my body just so, I managed to wedge myself into a reasonable, though rigid, catnap position. *Man—almost perfect if I'd ordered that quick-release racer's steering wheel.* Chris tells of horrifying other drivers by repositioning one at stoplights.

After waking, an hour later, I wandered over to the inspection area. Half a dozen vehicles were lined up in front of drive-in garage bays, with an equal number of empty trailers parked nearby. *Was I the only guy to have driven his car here?* Apparently, but I alone knew that, since you couldn't tell which trailer belonged to which auto.

Many of the vehicles were "replicars," reproductions of classic MGs and Mercedes. A dune buggy awaited inspection, too, and a three-wheeled motorcycle that appeared to be half Harley, half Beetle. The drivers—all men—talked shop, mostly concerning their dodges (of government authority).

Replica Auburn owner: "So this fellow puts silicone spray on the windshield of his regular car, where the emission sticker's gonna go. He wants to drive the other one, he moves the sticker over."

Gazelle driver: "Oklahoma, that's what someone told me—you can register by mail. Or was it Kansas? There's a whole book tells you how to do it."

Dune-buggy teenager: "Shoot, cost me more to get it legal than the car's worth. Yeah, like $900."

The Seven proved, no thanks to me, one of the better-made automobiles.

One car flew clear out of the inspection shed before stopping dead; the emergency brake was defunct. My handbrake did function, that day at least, if only because I knew exactly how hard I needed to pull on it—two clicks and the brake wouldn't hold, four and it was almost impossible to disengage. Another car was making a repeat trip to Wethersfield, blackballed previously for inadequate seat bolts; the Seven passed this inspection, which means Nader hasn't driven a Seven, lately.

The examiners shook their heads over the dune buggy and the three-wheeler, and you could practically hear them grumble *junkyard jalopies*. The Seven, by contrast, they treated with kid gloves. Yes, it applies to cars as well: If you look good, you're presumed good, and receive the benefit of the doubt.

The Seven's front-wheel alignment—surprise, surprise—was way off . . . so bad, in fact, that the DMV scale couldn't measure *how* bad. The inspector said he'd overlook the problem, though, undoubtedly assuming a Seven owner had both the desire and wherewithal to fix it. He also pointed out a possible fluid leak—evidence of the oil-cooler break?—but the problem was not, apparently, a mandatory fail.

We had passed. The Seven was legal!

I drove home in broad daylight, and of clear conscience,

for the first time. On the freeway I considered passing a semi by driving underneath it, but didn't.

A few weeks later I drove to Cambridge for the Seven's final checkout. I had timed the trip to coincide with a Seven-owner gathering organized by Chris, so when I arrived at the shop a number were already parked in front. One was black, another green, a third all silver, but most looked dismayingly familiar: silver body with red fiberglass wings and black interior. Most were a year or three older than mine, some went back a decade or more, and their owners eagle-eyed every incoming car, wondering how their babies measured up. One couple left their Seven HPC home—understandably, they lived on the West Coast—but passed around, like proud parents, a photo album of their beloved's birth.

When I showed Chris my baby, the first thing he said was "ooooooh." Within two seconds he'd spotted a mistake: I had mounted the hood medallion too far forward on the nose cone. To hide my embarrassment I asked Chris about wheel alignment, and a few minutes later he was on his knees beside my car. More owners gathered as Chris brandished a pair of mirror-bearing, L-shaped metal frames; they were delighted to witness an alignment properly done.

One onlooker, though, considered the task old hat. Jeff had bought a Lotus Seven in England more than twenty years earlier and still owned the car, still raced it. He said, after running a hand across my right-front wheel, "Already feathered." I checked, and Jeff was right; the individual treads were slightly higher on one side.

I had driven my roadster less than three hundred miles.

Chris completed his inspection the next day, at a Seven picnic twenty miles west of Boston. The procession must have been amazing to see; nearly a dozen noisy, insectlike, apparently old cars cruising through rural Massachusetts, every driver with a smile on his face.

The picnic took place, fortuitously, at Fruitlands—the farm where some of Thoreau's closest friends (including Bronson Alcott, father of Louisa May) attempted to establish, in 1843, a Transcendentalist utopia. The swift demise of Fruitlands was one inspiration for Thoreau's move to Walden the following year; the utopia's failure demonstrated that nature must be understood on her own terms.

I couldn't help wondering, as Chris clambered behind the wheel to test-drive my Seven, whether Thoreau would disdain my project or grudgingly admire it.

Chris's inspection was minimal. The throttle was sticky, he noted, the right-rear suspension creaky, the oil low—the pressure-gauge needle dropped significantly during cornering. No other problems manifested themselves, however, and the just-diagnosed ones took ten minutes to fix: I had remembered the tool kit, this time, and had brought two quarts of oil as well. The suspension creak couldn't be repaired right then, but Chris at least fingered its cause—I had probably tightened a bushing before it was fully loaded.

I didn't dare ask Chris to grade my build, though I divined a gentleman's C. I hadn't gotten a C since freshman linguistics, when I neglected to hand in the term paper—but hey, the Seven ran, and ran well, and no one could tell me different.

17

SPEED RACER

Racing was not foremost in my mind, or even aftmost, when I decided to build the Seven. That's the primary goal of many Seven owners, of course, but my driving pleasures lay in the sense of freedom, of being part of the landscape, not speed or conquest. Lisa and Thea and I attended a Seven race at the Brands Hatch track a few days after my Caterham visit, but the experience didn't inspire me to purchase a helmet. The racing was exciting, turn-of-the-century primitive, but awfully noisy and not exactly family oriented. Thea, eighteen months old, spent much of the day with her hands clamped over her ears, and I could imagine her watching Daddy miss a turn, clip another Seven, and . . .

Chris, by contrast, was a race booster. He built Sevens

not for the fun of it—the beginner's mind lay decades in his past—but to serve his track addiction. It was in his blood: Chris had spent years in the Bahamas—his father, a former captain in the Polish navy, was appointed Freeport's harbormaster in the 1960s—when Grand Bahama was known for road racing. Chris arrived after the demise of the famous Nassau Speed Weeks, but the island's sports-car culture was still very much alive.

"Great weather, everyone was young and single and knew everyone else," Chris recalls, "and you had to have a sports car"—even if the roads were crushed coral.

A few years earlier, back in Britain, Chris had been a teenage entrepreneur, refurbishing and reselling clapped-out automobiles. He continued the business in the Caribbean, but Chris soon drifted into the local racing scene. As a founding member of the Bahamas' sports-car club, he spent most of his leisure time—after "putting fifteen thousand miles a year on cars going nowhere" for the harbor authority—playing with automobiles. He raced in Freeport's Formula V series; flew to Sebring with friends to be a volunteer race marshal ("we allotted a case of beer per person per day"); drove in Jamaica's thousand-mile, round-the-island rally. The footloose years didn't last, of course, ending soon after a blind date. Chris and Mari, newlyweds, moved to Massachusetts in 1984 for the sake of Mari's career . . . after a quick detour, for Chris, to England.

"There I was," says Chris, "free use of a friend's London apartment, a wife in the U.S., and no prospects." He started looking for car-related employment in America, and naturally went to the Caterham works. Chris knew about Lotus and the Seven—once owned a Lotus Cortina for three weeks, until an acquaintance totaled it—and Graham Nearn, as it happened, was concerned about U.S. sales. The existing New England dealer had begun producing unauthorized Sevens under his own marque, which did not make Nearn happy.

"See what you can do," Nearn told Chris, and within a few years he was selling a score of Sevens annually.

Chris likes the car business, the deal making and horse-trading, but clearly prefers the track. "Dicing" with another car through curves and straightaways; pushing a Seven to, and past, its limits; recounting tall tales of hair-raising near-misses, miraculous comebacks, idiotic maneuvers, personal records—Chris's enthusiasm was catching, and eventually I caught the bug. "You should try it, you're missing something," said Chris, and he was right.

My first race, an autocross, was not optimally timed. I had been in California the previous evening, so I drove to the track—a huge college-campus parking lot with a cone-marked course—almost directly from the airport. My Seven was already on hand: Chris had picked it up in Brookfield the previous day, having paid my entry fee in exchange for letting him use the car as a demonstrator. Chris had already posted some good times in the Seven, and I wouldn't come close to matching them; indeed, during each of my three runs I earned not numbers but the chastening letters DNF, for Did Not Finish.

I thought I'd completed the course, but apparently hadn't followed it correctly. I saw the layout on paper, watched a few autocrossers run the route, registered the location of the straightaways and hairpins and S-turns . . . but was frequently unsure, once in the car, of my next move. *Man, how can you see anything when you're so close to the ground?! Shit, which of those cones marks the lane? Is it clockwise into the roundabout, or counterclockwise?* To this day I don't know whether my problems were caused by jet lag or nerves, poor track markings or simple ineptitude.

I returned to Lime Rock a few weeks later, this time as a paid-up competitor in the national Lotus club's Track Day. I had left Brookfield with trepidation—I was tempted, seeing the morning drizzle, to stay home—but decided that familiar faces, and familiar cars, would put me at ease. Numerous Sevens would be in action, and many of the Lotuses would be decades old; my car, theoretically, should be one of the most reliable.

I signed up for the novice group, and stood along the rail as the advanced-class drivers aligned themselves on the starting grid. The pace car, confoundingly, was a Volkswagen Vanagon, but it ran the course with aplomb. The VW's driver demonstrated, to my rookie eyes, a good line through the course, then pulled into the pit lane. The Lotuses immediately had at it, their owners respecting, for the most part, the track's "no passing, no racing" rules.

I borrowed a helmet—from David, owner of the first Seven I'd driven—in the nick of time for the novice run. I pulled into the grid toward the front of the pack, and while awaiting the start-your-engines signal schmoozed and gossiped, complained and compared, with the other drivers.

Phil, so big he hardly fit in a Seven, volunteered that he wasn't really a novice. "Thought I'd start out slow today, it's been a while. And there are some real jerks on the track—that white Elan in the intermediates? He's gonna kill somebody."

"A collector," acknowledged another man with a nod, using the term for racers who "collect" other cars by hitting them.

Frank, a lawyer: "Every year it's someone. Bet he'll end up in the weeds—I just hope he doesn't take anyone else with him."

The nervous chatter helped us get loose. But not too loose; our first few laps were sedate, we novices wanting to hit the turns just so without tailgating the drivers ahead of us or slowing those behind.

Nine track runs were scheduled—three for each of the

three race-ability classes—but many drivers, the beginners in particular, were satisfied with one. Perhaps fifteen cars participated in the first novice event; by the second the number was down to a dozen, and by the third, six.

What we lost in quantity, though, we made up for in quality. The remaining drivers were more competitive, less cautious, and in higher-powered cars; the foolhardy—those of us still on the track—had been separated from the sensible. We experienced novices—now there's a contradiction—had witnessed spinouts, missed turns, flying dirt, angry words, and near accidents among the other drivers; and by golly, we wanted to test our limits, too.

In the paddock before my last run I made the mistake of asking an acquaintance, an auto engineer who owned a green, late-model Elan, if he was enjoying the advanced-class driving.

"Yeah," he said. "But I lost time to that '75 Elite, he hit the apex early and shifted down right in front—I almost got pranged from behind. And the car seemed real flat at 6,000; I don't think the BHPs are quite what they say. I had to throw it around because of the understeer, and the rear end was always tramping."

That's approximately what he said, at least, for in truth he spoke a language that struck my ears like Greek.

We six novices, having taken the final start flag, quickly divided into two clusters. The front group didn't contain a single authentic Lotus: My car was a Caterham, of course, the others a TVR and a race-ready Camaro. Non-Lotus vehicles were permitted when the owners pled—and who could doubt it?—that their Lotuses were out of commission.

The Camaro, black, took off like a bat out of hell, the driver reckless and nothing like a novice. The yellow TVR stayed right on his tail, with me in distant pursuit.

We had completed only a single lap when things went

ragged. Attempting to catch the Camaro in the Esses, the TVR spun out and stopped cold maybe two car lengths ahead of me. I had to run into the dirt to avoid a collision, but got back on the asphalt without incident. I later learned the TVR owner wasn't a novice, either; he had previously learned, at Lime Rock's driving school, the "feet to the floor" (brake and clutch) emergency control technique. I was about the only novice, it seemed, in the final novice run.

By the third lap, the lead group had decided the no-passing, no-racing rules were for wimps. It was every man for himself now, each of us dedicated to hitting the apexes just right, cutting a second or two off our best lap times . . . and, yes, beating the other guy to the checkered flag.

I resolved to push where the Seven was most responsive, in the turns; that was the only way to make up the ground we lost in the straightaways. We had already lapped the remaining Elan and Elite, those cars laboring (I was subsequently told) from overheating and brake fade, but the Seven was going from strength to strength. Although I couldn't get 100 mph out of her on Back Straight, the Seven was smooth as silk through the curves and grades.

By this time I was using the entire track, as I'd been instructed—cutting into corners late and hard, and slingshotting out of them fast enough to be hurled to the far side of the course. In three places I was having great fun: in the Esses, throwing the car quickly left, quickly right; at West Bend, an uphill turn on top of which you almost left the ground; at Diving Turn, where you floored the accelerator (in anticipation of Back Straight) and experienced NASA-caliber g-forces. In two places I was having trouble: at the end of Back Straight, where I braked too early for fear of losing adhesion in the upcoming turn, and through Big Bend itself, which didn't seem to offer a single good line.

I didn't lose control of the Seven until my final lap. On an earlier circuit I almost had to bail into Back Straight's escape lane, having braked too late to negotiate Big Bend cleanly, but at the last second found an adequate line. Not this time, though; as the TVR sprinted through the Esses ahead of me I fishtailed far left, then far right after overcorrecting. I would have panicked except that nothing else happened; no spinout, no sense of almost-roll, no further loss of traction.

The white flag went up, and I spotted it with mixed feelings—glad to give my adrenal gland a rest, but still hoping to wear it out.

Two weeks later the Seven broke down again. It backfired a mile from home, the engine going *pfffft pop* and a puff of smoke issuing from the carburetors. I pulled over, thinking the problem no more than a severe engine miss, but the car hesitated badly after I started up again.

Vapor lock, or a nearly empty gas tank? A fill-up didn't help: The engine ran progressively worse, until the tach registered 6,000 rpm in neutral and refused to fall. I pulled over again, hoping to make an on-the-fly repair, but saw, when I removed the bonnet, rubber jutting from the back of the nearest carburetor. *A blown gasket*—which translated, without further thought, into *tow truck*.

The problem seemed serious. When I took off the faulty carburetor, back home, I discovered that its auxiliary venturi, made of aluminum, had melted . . . and in liquid form dripped back into the carb body, where it had transformed, on cooling, into a miniature Halloween mask. There it blocked open the butterfly-valve throttle, which is operated by the accelerator pedal: That explained the engine's uncontrollable racing.

"Looks like an engine fire," said Chris, after I sent him the impaired carburetor. "Could have been a major backfire, or maybe the gasket went first. I'll tell you this—it got hot in there!"

Chris sent back the carburetor with a new venturi and a new filter, and three weeks later I was on the road again . . . though not with the confidence I had once enjoyed.

Time to sell the Seven?

The question crossed my mind. The odometer had clocked less than a thousand miles, and already I'd had two breakdowns. On the other hand, the problems had occurred within the Seven's run-in period: I shouldn't jump to conclusions, lay blame too casually.

Forget it, for now at least. Deal with things, right?

For that was the central point. Getting rid of the Seven, in the wake of a mechanical setback, was a cop-out; a self-indulgent cream-skimming, a refusal to live with mistakes—the majority yet to be discovered, no doubt, and mine alone. I had learned a lot while building the Seven . . . but repairing it, wouldn't that be even more instructive?

George Sturt, a turn-of-the-century wheelwright, explains. While "new-work," he wrote,

> was largely controlled by proven theories and by well-tried
> fashions . . . repairs called for ingenuity, adaptiveness,
> readiness to make shift. It wasn't quite enough to know how
> to do this or that; you needed also to know something about
> the why, and to be ready to think of alternative dodges for
> improvising a temporary effect. . . .

Repair work, "dodges": That'd test my resourcefulness, compel me to dig even deeper. Was I up to the task, or was I going to walk away?

Zing!

Huh. *There goes that Y chromosome again. . . .*

FURTHER READING

Considering the influence of the automobile on modern life, it's surprising how few first-rate books have been written on the subject. An exception is James Flink's *The Automobile Age*, which I seemed to refer to every other day; I turned to countless other volumes as well, but a disproportionate number tended toward the polemical or celebratory and were thus of limited use. The list below is by no means confined to the automotive field; I cite most of the books I read in preparing this one, and a handful I only consulted, because I have doubtless absorbed and reproduced, amoebalike, numerous ideas and insights I didn't originate.

Most documented facts and quotations cited in the text can be found in one of the following books. (The exceptions, as a rule, are motor-industry statistics, which I have derived either from the *New York Times, Road & Track, Car and Driver, Autoweek,* or *Lotus reMarque*—the very fine newsletter of the Lotus Owners Group— and a few British car magazines.) The first few drafts of this manuscript carried a hundred-odd source notes, but after much consideration I have eliminated specific citations—for the sake of readability, yes, but also to avoid being mistaken for an expert on anything. Some of the books (and a few articles) listed below do speak with deserved authority; others proved equally helpful for their passion, imagination, or sheer eccentricity.

Adams, Henry. 1961 (1918). *The Education of Henry Adams.* Boston: Houghton Mifflin.

Altshuler, Alan, Martin Anderson, Daniel Jones, Daniel Ross, James Womack, and others. 1985. *The Future of the Automobile: The Report of MIT's International Automobile Program*. Cambridge, MA: The MIT Press.

American Automobile Manufacturers Association. 1997. *Motor Vehicle Facts & Figures, 1997*. Detriot, MI: AAMA.

Arnold, Graham. 1986. *The Illustrated Lotus Buyer's Guide*. Osceola, WI: Motorbooks International.

———. 1984. *Lotus Seven Super Profile*. Newbury Park, California: Haynes Publications/Foulis Motoring Books.

Asher, Robert, and Ronald Edsforth, ed. 1995. *Autowork*. Albany, NY: The State University of New York Press.

Bardou, Jean-Pierre, Jean-Jacques Chanaron, Patrick Fridenson, James M. Laux, translated by James M. Laux. 1982. *The Automobile Revolution: The Impact of an Industry*. Chapel Hill, NC: The University of North Carolina Press.

Bell, Daniel. 1960. "Work and Its Discontents: The Cult of Efficiency in America," in *The End of Ideology*. New York: The Free Press.

Berg, Ivan. 1992. *Guinness World Car Record*. Osceola, WI: Motorbooks International.

Berger, K. T. 1993. *Where the Road and the Sky Collide*. New York: Henry Holt.

———. 1988. *Zen Driving*. New York: Ballantine Books.

Burke, James. 1978. *Connections*. Boston: Little, Brown and Company.

———. 1996. *The Pinball Effect: How Renaissance Water Gardens Made the Carburetor Possible*. Boston: Little, Brown and Company.

Burlingame, Roger. 1954. *Henry Ford*. New York: Signet Books.

Bury, J. B. 1987 (1932). *The Idea of Progress: An Inquiry into Its Origins and Growth*. Mineola, NY: Dover Publications.

Calabresi, Guido. 1985. *Ideals, Beliefs, Attitudes, and the Law*. Syracuse, NY: Syracuse University Press.

Carrazé, Alain, Hélène Oswald, and others, translated by Christine Donougher. 1989. *The Prisoner: A Televisionary Masterpiece*. London: W.H. Allen/Virgin.

Clarke, R. M. 1989. *Lotus & Caterham Seven Gold Portfolio, 1957–1989*. Cobham, Surrey: Brooklands Books.

Coulter, Jeremy. 1986. *The Lotus & Caterham Sevens: A Collector's Guide*. Croydon, England: Motor Racing Publications Ltd.

Coxhead, Peter, and Martin Foster. 1990. *The Kitcar Builder's Manual: Buying, Building, Trimming*. Sparkford, Somerset: Haynes Publishing/Foulis Motoring Books.

Crombac, Gerard. 1986. *Colin Chapman: The Man and His Cars*. Wellingborough, England: Patrick Stephens Limited.

Csikszentmihalyi, Mihaly. 1990. *Flow: The Psychology of Optimal Experience*. New York: Harper & Row.

Dauphinais, Dean D., and Peter M. Gareffa. 1996. *Car Crazy: The Official Motor City High-Octane, Turbocharged, Chrome-Plated, Back Road Book of Car Culture*. Detroit: Visible Ink Press.

Doray, Bernard, translated by David Macey. 1988. *From Taylorism to Fordism: A Rational Madness*. London: Free Association Books.

Durkheim, Emile, translated by George Simpson. 1964 (1933). *The Division of Labor in Society*. New York: The Free Press.

Edwards, John. 1993. *Auto Dictionary*. Los Angeles: HP Books.

Ellul, Jacques, translated by John Wilkinson. 1964. *The Technological Society*. New York: Vintage Books.

Emerson, Ralph Waldo. 1993 (1841). "Self-Reliance," in *Self-Reliance and Other Essays*. Mineola, NY: Dover Publications.

Feldman, Richard, and Michael Betzold. 1988. *End of the Line: Autoworkers and the American Dream*. New York: Weidenfeld & Nicolson.

Finch, Christopher. 1992. *Highways to Heaven: The AUTObiography of America*. New York: HarperCollins.

Ford, Henry, with Samuel Crowther. 1923. *My Life and Work*. Garden City, NY: Doubleday, Page & Company.

Flink, James J. 1990. *The Automobile Age*. Cambridge: The MIT Press.

Forster, E. M. 1985 (1915). *Howard's End*. New York: Bantam Books.

———. 1952 (1924). *A Passage to India*. New York: Harcourt, Brace & World.

Gartman, David. 1986. *Auto Slavery: The Labor Process and the American Automobile Industry, 1897–1950*. New Brunswick, NJ: Rutgers University Press.

Gelderman, Carol. 1981. *Henry Ford: The Wayward Capitalist.* New York: St. Martin's Press.

Gies, Frances & Joseph. 1994. *Cathedral, Forge, and Waterwheel: Technology and Invention in the Middle Ages.* New York: HarperCollins.

Gilbreth, Frank B., Jr., and Ernestine Gilbreth Carey. 1950. *Belles on Their Toes.* New York: Bantam Books.

———. *Cheaper by the Dozen.* 1948. New York: Bantam Books.

Goodrich, Chris. 1991. *Anarchy and Elegance: Confessions of a Journalist at Yale Law School.* Boston: Little, Brown and Company.

de Grazia, Sebastian. 1962. *Of Time, Work, and Leisure.* New York: Anchor Books.

Halberstam, David. 1986. *The Reckoning.* New York: William Morrow and Company.

Hamper, Ben. 1991. *Rivethead: Tales from the Assembly Line.* New York: Warner Books.

Hardin, Garrett. 1968. "The Tragedy of the Commons," *Science,* vol. 162, pp. 1243–48.

Haskell, Hugh. 1993. *Colin Chapman, Lotus Engineering: Theories, Designs & Applications.* London: Osprey Automotive.

Hawke, David Freeman. 1988. *Nuts and Bolts of the Past: A History of American Technology, 1776–1860.* New York: Harper & Row.

Heilbroner, Robert L. 1953. *The Worldly Philosophers: The Lives, Times, and Ideas of the Great Economic Thinkers.* New York: Simon & Schuster.

Hobsbawn, E.J. 1968. *Industry and Empire.* London: Penguin Books.

Hora, Max. 1987. *Village World: The World of "The Prisoner" Further Explored.* Ipswich, England: Six of One/The Prisoner Appreciation Society

Huxley, Aldous. 1950 (1932). *Brave New World.* London: Penguin Books.

Ingrassia, Paul, and Joseph B. White. 1994. *Comeback: The Fall & Rise of the American Automobile Industry.* New York: Simon & Schuster.

Illich, Ivan, Irving Kenneth Zola, John McKnight, Jonathan Kaplan, and Harley Shaiken. 1977. *Disabling Professions.* London: Marion Boyars Publishers.

Illich, Ivan. 1978. *Toward a History of Needs*. New York: Pantheon Books.

Jacobs, Jane. 1961. *The Death and Life of Great American Cities*. New York: Vintage Books.

Jerome, John. 1996 (1977). *Truck: On Rebuilding a Worn-Out Pickup and Other Post-Technological Adventures*. Hanover, NH: University Press of New England.

Kanigel, Robert. 1997. *The One Best Way: Frederick Winslow Taylor and the Enigma of Efficiency*. New York: The Viking Press.

Kay, Jane Holtz. 1997. *Asphalt Nation: How the Automobile Took Over America and How We Can Take It Back*. New York: Crown Publishers.

Keller, Maryann. 1989. *Rude Awakening: The Rise, Fall, and Struggle for Recovery of General Motors*. New York: HarperPerennial.

———. 1993. *Collision: GM, Volkswagen, and the Race to Own the 21st Century*. New York: Doubleday Currency.

Kuhn, Thomas S. 1970. *The Structure of Scientific Revolutions*, 2nd ed. Chicago: The University of Chicago Press.

Lamm, Jay. 1992. *How to Restore British Sports Cars*. Osceola, WI: Motorbooks International.

Lasch, Christopher. 1991. *The True and Only Heaven: Progress and Its Critics*. New York: W.W. Norton.

Lewis, Daniel L., and Lawrence Goldstein, editors. 1983. *The Automobile and American Culture*. Ann Arbor: The University of Michigan Press.

McLellan, David. 1990. *Utopian Pessimist: The Life and Thought of Simone Weil*. New York: Poseidon Press.

McShane, Clay. 1994. *Down the Asphalt Path: The Automobile and the American City*. New York: Columbia University Press.

Marx, Karl. 1978 (1867). *Das Kapital*, excerpts from *The Marx-Engels Reader*, 2nd ed., edited by Robert C. Tucker. New York: W.W. Norton.

Marx, Leo. 1964. *The Machine in the Garden: Technology and the Pastoral Ideal in America*. New York: Oxford University Press.

Mirsky, Jeannette, and Allan Nevins. 1952. *The World of Eli Whitney*. New York: The Macmillan Company.

Morland, Andrew. 1994. *Lotus Seven and Caterham*. London: Osprey Automotive.

Nadis, Steve, and James J. MacKenzie. 1993. *Car Trouble*. Boston: Beacon Press.

Nelson, Walter Henry. 1970. *Small Wonder: The Amazing Story of the Volkswagen*. Boston: Little, Brown and Company.

Pétrement, Simone, translated by Raymond Rosenthal. 1976. *Simone Weil: A Life*. New York: Pantheon Books.

Petroski, Henry. 1992. *The Pencil: A History of Design and Circumstance*. New York: Alfred A. Knopf.

———. 1985. *To Engineer Is Human: The Role of Failure in Successful Design*. New York: St. Martin's Press.

Pirsig, Robert M. 1974. *Zen and the Art of Motorcycle Maintenance: An Inquiry into Values*. New York: Bantam Books.

Rabinbach, Anson. 1990. *The Human Motor: Energy, Fatigue, and the Origins of Modernity*. New York: BasicBooks.

Rae, John B. 1965. *The American Automobile: A Brief History*. Chicago: The University of Chicago Press.

Richardson, Robert D., Jr. 1986. *Henry David Thoreau: A Life of the Mind*. Berkeley, CA: The University of California Press.

Rifkin, Jeremy. 1987. *Time Wars: The Primary Conflict in Human History*. New York: Touchstone/Simon & Schuster.

———. 1995. *The End of Work: The Decline of the Global Labor Force and the Dawn of the Post-Market Era*. New York: Jeremy P. Tarcher/Putnam.

Rogers, Dave. 1989. *The Prisoner: The Authorised History of the Adventures of No. 6*. New York: Barnes & Noble Books.

Rybczynski, Witold. 1983. *Taming the Tiger: The Struggle to Control Technology*. New York: Penguin Books.

Sale, Kirkpatrick. 1995. *Rebels Against the Future: The Luddites and Their War on the Industrial Revolution*. Reading, MA: Addison-Wesley.

Schor, Juliet B. 1992. *The Overworked American: The Unexpected Decline of Leisure*. New York: BasicBooks.

Shaiken, Harley. 1984. *Work Transformed: Automation & Labor in the Computer Age*. New York: Holt, Rinehart and Winston.

Sherman, Joe. 1994. *In the Rings of Saturn*. New York: Oxford University Press.

Sloan, Alfred P., Jr., with Boyden Sparkes. 1941. *Adventures of a White-Collar Man*. New York: Doubleday, Doran & Company.

Sloan, Alfred P., Jr., edited by John McDonald with Catharine Stevens. 1964. *My Years with General Motors*. Garden City, NY: Doubleday & Company.

Smith, Adam. 1986 (1776). *The Wealth of Nations*, excerpts from *The Essential Adam Smith*, edited by Robert Heilbroner. New York: W.W. Norton.

Snow, C. P. 1959. *The Two Cultures*. Cambridge: Cambridge University Press.

Smith, Carroll. 1990. *Nuts, Bolts, Fasteners and Plumbing Handbook*. Osceola, WI: Motorbooks International.

Sturt, George. 1973. *The Wheelwright's Shop*. Cambridge: Cambridge University Press.

Suzuki, Shunryu. 1970. *Zen Mind, Beginner's Mind: Informal Talks on Zen Meditation and Practice*. New York: Weatherhill, Inc.

Tawney, R. H. 1948 (1920). *The Acquisitive Society*. New York: Harcourt, Brace, Jovanovich.

Taylor, Frederick Winslow. 1967 (1911). *The Principles of Scientific Management*. New York: W.W. Norton.

Thoreau, Henry David. 1960 (1854). *Walden and Civil Disobedience*, edited by Sherman Paul. Boston: Houghton Mifflin Company.

Tipler, John. 1995. *Lotus and Caterham Seven: Racers for the Road*. Ramsbury, Marlborough: The Crowood Press.

Twain, Mark. 1961 (1883). *Life on the Mississippi*. New York: Signet Books.

Veblen, Thorstein. 1948. *The Portable Veblen*, edited by Max Lerner. New York: The Viking Press.

———. 1994 (1899). *The Theory of the Leisure Class*. Mineola, NY: Dover Publications.

Weale, Tony. 1991. *Lotus Seven: Restoration, Preparation, Maintenance*. London: Osprey Automotive.

White, Matthew, and Jaffer Ali. 1988. *The Official Prisoner Companion*. New York: Warner Books.

Watkins, Monty. 1993. *How to Build a Kit Car*. Reigate, Surrey: Pineloft Ltd.

Williams, Heathcote. 1991. *Autogeddon*. New York: Arcade Publishing.

Williams-Ellis, Clough. 1971. *Architect Errant*. Portmeirion, Wales: Portmeirion Limited.

Wright, J. Patrick. 1979. *On a Clear Day You Can See General Motors: John Z. De Lorean's Look Inside the Automotive Giant.* New York: Avon Books.

Yates, Brock. 1984. *The Decline & Fall of the American Automobile Industry.* New York: Vintage Books.

Zuckerman, Wolfgang. 1991. *End of the Road: The World Car Crisis and How We Can Solve It.* Post Mills, VT: Chelsea Green Publishing.